HOMESCHOOLING

HOMESCHOOLING

A Family's Journey

- - - - - - -

Gregory and Martine Millman

JEREMY P. TARCHER/PENGUIN
a member of Penguin Group (USA) Inc.
New York

JEREMY P. TARCHER/PENGUIN
Published by the Penguin Group
Penguin Group (USA) Inc., 375 Hudson Street, New York, New York 10014, USA •
Penguin Group (Canada), 90 Eglinton Avenue East, Suite 700, Toronto,
Ontario M4P 2Y3, Canada (a division of Pearson Canada Inc.) • Penguin Books Ltd,
80 Strand, London WC2R 0RL, England • Penguin Ireland, 25 St Stephen's Green,
Dublin 2, Ireland (a division of Penguin Books Ltd) • Penguin Group (Australia),
250 Camberwell Road, Camberwell, Victoria 3124, Australia (a division of
Pearson Australia Group Pty Ltd) • Penguin Books India Pvt Ltd, 11 Community
Centre, Panchsheel Park, New Delhi–110 017, India • Penguin Group (NZ),
67 Apollo Drive, Rosedale, North Shore 0632, New Zealand (a division of
Pearson New Zealand Ltd) • Penguin Books (South Africa) (Pty) Ltd, 24 Sturdee
Avenue, Rosebank, Johannesburg 2196, South Africa

Penguin Books Ltd, Registered Offices: 80 Strand, London WC2R 0RL, England

Most Tarcher/Penguin books are available at special quantity discounts for bulk purchase for sales promotions, premiums, fund-raising, and educational needs. Special
books or book excerpts also can be created to fit specific needs. For details, write
Penguin Group (USA) Inc. Special Markets, 375 Hudson Street, New York, NY 10014.

Library of Congress Cataloging-in-Publication Data

Millman, Gregory.
Homeschooling : a family's journey / Gregory and Martine Millman.
p.   cm.
Includes bibliographical references and index.
ISBN 978-1-58542-661-4
1. Home schooling—United States.   I. Millman, Martine.   II. Title.
LC40.M55   2008   2008018350
371.04'2—dc22

Printed in the United States of America
1   3   5   7   9   10   8   6   4   2

Book design by Michelle McMillian

While the authors have made every effort to provide accurate telephone numbers and
Internet addresses at the time of publication, neither the publisher nor the authors
assume any responsibility for errors, or for changes that occur after publication.
Further, the publisher does not have any control over and does not assume any
responsibility for author or third-party websites or their content.

With gratitude, we dedicate this book to
our parents and first teachers:

Edith and Gail Parmer
and
Celeste and William Millman.

Thank you.

Contents

We have done so much, for so long, with so little,
we are now qualified to do anything with nothing.

—MOTHER TERESA

Introduction

Homeschooling is the Silicon Valley of American education. It's all about freedom, innovation, autonomy, self-organization, and creative collaboration. Researchers report that homeschoolers not only score, on average, well above the conventionally schooled when they take standardized tests but also participate in more extracurricular activities, communicate better, have a more diverse range of social contacts, and are better socialized and more mature than the conventionally schooled.[1] Homeschoolers "are the epitome of Brown students," Associate Dean Joyce Reed of Brown University has said. "They are self-directed, they take risks, and they don't back off."[2] Other college admissions officers interviewed for this book generally agreed.

When we began to homeschool, in the early 1990s, it was a risky choice. Around the country, homeschoolers still had to worry about being charged with truancy and perhaps even having their children taken away. Now, though, homeschooling is legal in every state (although regulations differ from state to state), and almost everyone knows someone who homeschools. In February 2007, a California court threatened homeschoolers in that state with a ruling that all children had to be taught by credentialed teachers. The governor called that ruling "outrageous," and even the state's superintendent of education defended the right to homeschool.[3] Shortly afterward, the court vacated its ruling and agreed to rehear the case in question.

Yet few people know what homeschooling is in practice. "I could never do that" is something we've often heard from people who are interested in homeschooling but intimidated by what they imagine is involved. Because they think homeschooling is impossible for them, some people leave children in mediocre, poor, and even downright dangerous schools. (The U.S. Department of Education's National Center for Education Statistics reports that 10 percent of urban schoolchildren fear being attacked at school.)[4] Sometimes people try to homeschool and encounter opposition from spouses, relatives, or friends who think homeschoolers need special qualifications and credentials.

In fact, homeschooling needn't be all that complicated. Most of the homeschooling parent's job is to coach and encourage, help a child develop good study habits, and show how to find answers to questions. It's not the homeschooling parent's job to know all the answers.

Teaching credentials don't matter in homeschooling. Teaching credentials prepare people to work within an institutional structure—the school system—that has nothing to do with homeschooling. In fact, the word "homeschooling" can be misleading, because it suggests that something like school happens in the home. But most homeschoolers don't do the same things that schools do. They succeed not because they do school things better but because they do better things than school. Homeschoolers can do one thing, especially, that schools cannot do: focus on the distinctive abilities and needs of each child, on each child's level of maturity, on each child's interests, on each teachable moment, and fit the educational system to the child instead of forcing the child to fit into a system.

This memoir shows, we hope, how that works in practice. We are a family of two parents, Martine and Gregory, and six homeschooled children: Bridget, Anna, and Magdalen (Lena), all now in college, and William (Billy), Joseph (Joey), and Blaise, who are still high school age or younger. This is a family's story, and every member of the family helped to write it. It presents every aspect of our homeschooling experience as thoroughly, as clearly, and as simply as we know how. (For the purposes of narrative convenience only, we tell most of the story from the point of view of one individual, whose first-person "I" should be considered that of a spokesperson for the family.)

- - - - - - -

ONE

Our Homeschool Choice

We were living in an apartment in Hoboken, New Jersey, when the first baby came. We had moved to the neighborhood before many people knew about its advantages. When we found our apartment there, Hoboken was just a poky little enclave a few minutes from Manhattan by the PATH train. There was almost no crime, except for godfather-style organized crime, which not only doesn't break into your place but sometimes even helps to keep the streets safe. Rents were a steal, with apartments available at half or less than what they'd cost in nearby Manhattan.

All the time she was working as an editor in the city, Martine commuted away from quiet and came back to quiet and didn't miss much, because nothing much happened in Hoboken during the day. Then she became a stay-at-home mom. The timing was uncanny. She spent her first months of stay-at-home motherhood surrounded by the smash and clang of pile drivers slamming steel beams to bedrock so new condos would have firm foundations. Hoboken had been discovered. It wasn't all bad news. Rents and prices were rising, so brokers and owners and real estate developers were making a lot of money. There were great new clubs and restaurants opening, too. We might have gone to some of them if things had been a little different.

But a baby changes nightlife. No matter who was playing at Maxwell's, ours was the same show: feeding and changing, feeding and changing. The apartment suddenly seemed a lot smaller, too. We looked at the fenced-in pen of weeds and cinders behind our building and noticed that it was not really a yard. That hadn't mattered to us before. Now it seemed obvious that a child should have some green place to play. There was a park in town, but it was a long walk from the apartment, littered with discarded bottles, and haunted by stray dogs. So we started house-hunting. We were thinking of fresh air, grass, trees, swing sets, and barbecue grills. Suburbia would be perfect for us. There was a hitch. We needed a place that we could afford on one income.

House-Hunting on One Income

However, the whole New York metropolitan area was in the midst of a real estate bubble. When we started our hunt, house prices were sky-high and strapping on their oxygen masks to climb even higher.

We were so cautious that one real estate agent, when I told her what we were looking for and what we could pay, laughed and said our budget might qualify us to buy a trailer on a slab on leased land, but not to count on her finding it. Another showed us a tiny cottage wedged between a power station and a railroad track, with high-tension wires humming above it, and a backyard taken up by three or four graves, complete with gravestones. It was, she admitted, a bit pricey for our budget but maybe if we *stretched* . . . After all, they said, our income would grow! The house would increase in value—in this bubble, houses were a sure bet to go up! There were all sorts of creative mortgage structures that would allow us to pay what we could afford in the early years, and then, when our income went up, pay more!

We were skeptical, though. It was the mid-1980s. Just a few years earlier, interest rates had been 20 percent. Whole industries had disappeared from America. The phrase "Rust Belt" had entered the language to describe what used to be the "Steel Belt." I was still at an early stage in my career, but I had twice experienced the effects of what Austrian economist Joseph Schumpeter had called "creative destruction" at two companies where I had worked. We were already stretching when we decided to live on one income so that Martine could be a full-time mother. In order to protect that choice, we wanted a house that we could not only afford on one income but could continue to afford even if that income disappeared for a while.

We learned an important lesson about this single-income lifestyle. It forced us to be contrarians. As anyone knows who has ever read an investing guide, the best investment strategies are contrarian. "Buy when there's blood in the streets," the sage contrarian advice goes. After a long search, we found that the only neighborhood in which we could afford to buy had blood in the streets, so we took the advice.

Plainfield was a gracious old central New Jersey burg, once dubbed the Queen City for its affluence and splendor. As late as the 1950s it was said to have boasted the greatest number of millionaires per capita of any town in the United States. It still had its own symphony orchestra and a Shakespeare Garden that exhibited specimens of every plant mentioned in the bard's plays and sonnets. The library displayed several racks of Sung and Qing dynasty Chinese cloisonné and porcelain and held a collection of art including three Winslow Homers and some original Audubons, in addition to shelves upon shelves of thousands of rare and wonderful books. But these were the ruins that wealth had left behind in its rush to go. Riots in 1967 had scared away the white rich, who had abandoned their mansions. When we went house-hunting during the great real estate bubble of the 1980s, prices were still low in Plainfield.

The town's reputation was so bad that some agents refused to show us houses there. Eventually, with the help of an emotionally disturbed woman who was working part-time for a local broker, and who seemed to have few, if any, other clients, we found an especially good bargain near a beautiful park, in a neighborhood of trim yards and owner-occupied homes, where we helped to pioneer reverse integration. Most of our neighbors were families with children, nurses and cops and preachers and civil servants and truck drivers. Some of the wives stayed home.

The house was a fixer-upper that we purchased as is. A reclusive and eccentric widower had lived in it among piles of old newspapers and a lifetime of accumulated debris. Surrounding the house was a jungle of brush that had once, long ago, been his wife's garden. It took us months to clear overgrown brush from the yard and do enough repairs to make the house livable. But the house had good bones. An old carpenter who lived just a few doors down the street had designed and built it in the Great Depression. We got to know him, and found that in our attitudes to borrowing and risk, we had a lot in common. Not only was this house sounder than a dollar, the price was such that we could probably weather whatever came our way economically.

There were trade-offs, of course. One reason that we could afford to buy was that Plainfield's public schools were terrible. The buildings were in fine shape, but many of the students didn't see much of the inside of them. They got off the school bus in the morning and made the connections they wanted to make and then you would see them walking in loose clusters back up the streets to wherever the party got rolling at eight A.M. Those who spent the day in the buildings often had an agenda other than study. So those who did want to study had plenty of distractions, and so did the teachers who might really have wanted to teach. Just about anything that can go wrong with urban schools had gone wrong or was going wrong with Plainfield's; things were going from bad to worse. Administrators cycled through a revolving door at the top. Teachers and other employees got beaten up. Students got shot. The schools at times seemed to be preparing children for prison life. In one notorious incident, third-graders were strip-searched.[1]

Our Yuppie Plan Derailed

We knew that the public schools would not be an option for us. But we thought that this would just be our starter home. If things went well, we planned to move again in three to five years, before we needed schools. Real estate prices were still rising, so we could sell at a higher price than we'd paid, roll into a better neighborhood with better schools, and live a normal yuppie life. It wasn't a bad plan, just an unworkable plan. Before we could make repairs to the house and move in, we found that we were expecting another child. Two months after we moved in, we discovered that the "child" would be "children." We were about to have twins. Then the business I was working for began to shut down.

Martine had just given birth to the twins in September 1987, the stock market crashed in October 1987, and I departed the company on January 6, 1988, leaving behind a skeleton staff that would soon be gone. We noticed that it was the Feast of the Epiphany, and looked for the revelation.

I sent out résumés, because that's what one does, but more than thirty thousand people were sending out résumés around the same time.[2] The résumés brought no response. In the meantime, someone introduced me to the owner of a small financial magazine specializing in exotic new markets. I had worked on some deals that were offbeat and interesting to derivative and currency and Third World debt traders, and I had written a few articles over the years. So I wrote one article for him on trial, and he asked for another. I began to get phone calls from magazines in London and elsewhere asking for similar articles. So one thing led to another, and before long I was writing freelance on financial markets for half a dozen magazines. It didn't pay much, but it covered the mortgage when there was blood in the streets.

Recognizing Risk, Making Trade-Offs

The income of a freelance writer is insecure, of course. But so was everything else. Corporations had provided the illusion of security, but after trusting that illusion three times, with three companies, each of which failed in its own way, it now seemed better to have no security, and know it without a doubt, than to have no security and yet live in the illusion that there was security. Many people, under the illusion that they had security, were blind to the danger of their financial choices, such as piling on debt. We decided it would be better to accept insecurity and manage the risk than to ignore insecurity and keep trusting in some company or other to do what so many companies were incapable of doing—namely, survive.

Fortunately, we had already made extremely cautious financial decisions. We had bought a house so cheaply that even after I lost my job, and was only getting a few freelance assignments now and then, we could continue to pay the mortgage. During the first year or so, Martine also did quite a bit of writing. We were able to back each other up as we got our new, home-based, freelance-writing business off the ground. As the children grew older, though, they demanded more attention. Since editors had a way of demanding attention just about the time that children did, she had to make a choice. She chose the children. Instead of writing, she took over the bookkeeping for the business so that I could focus only on the work, rather than worry about the money we were or were not making and the bills that we needed to pay.

Fortunately, the late 1980s and early 1990s were good times for financial journalism, with numerous magazines opening and demanding copy. None of this ever actually amounted to security, of course. Journalism is surely among the more insecure professions in America. Many of the magazines that opened in the early 1990s were out of business a few years later. We had some exhilarating financial highs and some terrifying financial lows, but we managed the risks by controlling what we spent. We managed, in our small and rather amateur way, to cope with economic insecurity better than a lot of the experts.

As a financial writer, I often interviewed financiers, executives, and government officials, and found many of them surprisingly uninformed about what was going on in their own banks, companies, and countries. The collapse of the Japanese stock market in 1990, the collapse of the European Monetary System, the collapse of companies and banks and even governments because of financial irresponsibility—all only underscored the risk one took by relying on experts to manage things well. This probably made us more disposed than we might otherwise have been to take the bold step of homeschooling. It's a step we wouldn't have taken, though, if we could have avoided it.

We started our home-based freelance business when our eldest daughter was a little over two years of age. On the advice of a pediatrician, we enrolled her in preschool at age three. When it was time to enroll her in school, we faced a quandary.

School Daze

Because our address put us in its territory, we were members of a Catholic parish with a beautiful and historic church building in one of the town's worst precincts. Junkies and dealers spent the nights perched on the low wall surrounding the church, and hookers turned tricks in the doorways of the school. Shortly after we joined, the pastor discovered that if he poured oil on the wall, the dealers wouldn't sit there, because they didn't want to mess up their clothes. It was a brilliant coup. The dealers moved their trade a block or two away and the rest of the action followed them. But the neighborhood was still a ruin, and while the church's elderly, frail, dwindling, dying members put what they could into the collection basket, it was barely enough to pay the bills. When we talked with the pastor about school for our children, he told us frankly that he wouldn't recommend the parish school, since it was about to close for good. On his suggestion, we joined a parish in an adjoining town, only a few blocks away.

Financially healthy, though by no means sound, this new parish relied on parental involvement, fundraising, and donations to keep a reasonably mediocre school from getting any worse. Like other parents, we served our regular tours of duty in the smoky bingo hall handing out cards, calling numbers, serving Cokes and burgers, or cleaning up after old ladies who talked with cigarette croaks and came to the hall with their rubber trolls, lucky charms, drink holders, and pocket flasks, hoping to leave with wads of cash. The attraction of Catholic bingo games in urban neighborhoods isn't the modest official prize but the incredibly rich side action that local entrepreneurs organize among the players. Now and then we would hear shouts and cheers from a corner of the bingo hall where no one had gotten "bingo." We learned that an astute bet on number combinations can pay many times what even the most consistent bingo winner collects officially.

In addition to their work as amateur bingo croupiers, parents also volunteered as playground monitors, or as classroom babysitters when the teachers went on break. Martine spent her classroom stints explaining lessons to children who were struggling to understand the explanation the teacher had given. She discovered that she could explain things so they understood, mainly by paying attention to them. She asked what they understood and what they didn't understand, she listened to their answers, and she used what they understood to explain what they didn't understand. That seems obvious, but it wasn't the way teachers taught at St. Joseph's School.

That the most important part of teaching seemed to be patient listening was not a widely shared or very welcome insight. It was edgy to encourage questions, and we would find out what a faux pas it was to press for answers. The school's pedagogical culture blended rigor and apathy in a toxic, if not intoxicating, cocktail. Whether it was at all typical of contemporary Catholic schools, I don't know. The administration built barriers to block parental involvement and communication, and worked steadily to lower expectations. We got our first hint of this fact when our daughter was in the first grade and scored in the sixtieth percentile on a national achievement test. We took that score as a warning and planned to do more to help her. But when we asked the teacher what kind of help she thought our daughter needed to improve she said, "Why would you want to improve her performance? She's above average, isn't she?"

A bout of chicken pox taught us the school rule that forbade a parent to pick up homework for a child who was out sick, because the teachers were afraid of infection spreading from papers a sick child touched. The policy may have been reasonable from a teacher's point of view. It was hard on sick children, though. They fell behind. When they returned to school, tired after a bout of sickness, they faced a backlog of the work that they had missed. They had only a few days to clear that backlog and submit those assignments for grading. Meanwhile, they also had to keep up with the current work assignments. That was rough because they had missed the lessons on which the current work was based, and the teacher usually was not available to discuss lessons, homework assignments, or test performance.

Worse, from our perspective, was the fact that seeing things as they really were and telling the truth about them was against the unwritten rules. The way to succeed academically here was to figure out what the teacher wanted and give it to her, true or not. For example, one of our twin kindergartners colored apples yellow and green, like the ones she saw in the market, and got marked down for it because the teacher had an idea that all apples should be red. Imagination was even more hazardous. Her sister colored a cow purple because her favorite poem began, "I never saw a purple cow." The teacher put a frowning-face mark on the assignment to make it clear how wrong it was to color a cow purple. Maybe she was the only child in her kindergarten class who had read that poem. Maybe the teacher had never read it, either. We never found out, because the teacher didn't discuss these things.

Like other parents, we accepted the situation as normal until we encountered an anomaly that forced us to admit that it was bizarre. After coming back to school from her bout of chicken pox, our second-grader had taken a test. When the teacher graded it, she marked a correct answer wrong. There was no doubt about the answer. It wasn't one of those gray, could-go-either-way questions. We assumed the teacher, overwhelmed and stressed and working hard to cope with all the pressures of her job, the crowded classes and the low pay and all of the other burdens on teachers, had simply slipped up. But our daughter had been doing her best, and the test score knocked her off the honor roll, something that she took seriously. She couldn't understand why she was being penalized, because after all she had answered the question correctly. We tried to arrange an appointment with the teacher, but the teacher did not return our call. Instead, she sent a message back to us through the school secretary to say that she was not available for an appointment and that she did not want to discuss the matter.

Puzzled, we naively persisted. One phone call led to another and eventually we were called into the principal's office. Not invited, or asked to drop by, but called in. What it means to be called into the principal's office can be completely clear only to one who has attended a Catholic school. In fact, probably not just any Catholic school would do. It would have to be an urban Catholic school in a somewhat run-down brick building that had started out cream-colored but darkened to soot after about a century of exposure to polluted air. The neighborhood has to be a little shabby, so you check to make sure you lock your car before walking through the one open gate in the chain-link fence and toward the side door. It seems no one uses the old front door anymore, but at the side there is a modern glass-and-steel door with a buzzer that you ring, and after a while it buzzes, so you pass through the door and see a long, narrow hallway stretching away from a steep flight of stairs. The principal's office is always on the top floor.

You mount the steep stairs, dragging your reluctant hand along polished wooden handrails held up by wrought iron, and debouch into an eerily quiet corridor. You see the principal's office from a distance, halfway down the corridor, with a child's desk ominously posed in the silent, dark hallway just outside the principal's door. How well I remembered it all. A wayward child called to the principal's office shuddered at the sight of that desk, at the doom of sitting and waiting for the principal's door to open. Torquemada's own guidelines had recommended that, as a preliminary to interrogation, the inquisitors show the instruments of torture to the accused, and then leave the wretch alone to steep in fear and suspense. That approach still worked as well as ever. My wife, who had never attended Catholic schools, could not feel the short hairs along her arms and neck curling and straightening again at the sight of that desk as I could. Although we went in together, I was alone. It took a deliberate effort to remind myself that I was no longer ten years old.

The principal, a bulky nun with cropped gray hair, a plain dress and sweater, and an expression as kindly and benevolent as the hood ornament on a Mack truck, greeted us with courteous impatience. We explained that we had come about the problem with the test. We were having some difficulty explaining to our daughter why a clearly correct answer should have been marked wrong. The principal looked at us with eyes of glittering condescension, and said, "Yes, the answer is correct. But that's a fourth-grade answer, and your daughter is only in the second grade. She isn't supposed to know that yet."

"Excuse me?"

"It wouldn't be fair to the other children if we gave her credit for the answer. You see, you are a devoted couple, married, and you help your daughter study, and there are children in the class whose parents are divorced, or who don't speak English. Your daughter is ahead of them because you work with her. It wouldn't be fair to the others if we gave her credit for what she knows as a result of that advantage."

My wife and I looked at each other. We already knew that the public schools were not an option for us. We also knew that we couldn't afford the classy private school that might have been affordable on two incomes, because we had chosen to live on one income. Now the principal had just made it very clear that the Catholic school could not be an option for us, either. By the time we got back into our car, we had decided to homeschool.

Yet there was nothing bold or rash about our decision to homeschool. There was nothing ideological about it. If we had any reasonable conventional and mainstream alternative, we might never have considered homeschooling. But our decisions about how we were going to live, especially the decision to live on one income, made the decision to homeschool both possible and inevitable.

We were among the earlier adopters of homeschooling, having started to homeschool at the beginning of the 1990s. We had one daughter in the second grade, and three younger children not yet in first grade. Our two youngest were still a few years from being born.

At the time, homeschoolers were still fighting legal battles; homeschooling was illegal in some states, and equated with child neglect by some social work agencies. Yet these battles seldom drew much press attention, because homeschooling was too marginal to merit ink or airtime.

We now realize that we must have laid the foundation for our determination to homeschool before our first child was born. We were, without knowing it, predisposed to become homeschoolers. One of the most portentous decisions we made on the road to homeschooling was the decision that our children should have a very costly "luxury": a full-time mom. It seemed to us that a two-income lifestyle, then the norm among families in our age and education bracket, would require our children to make a sacrifice we didn't want to demand of them—namely, the sacrifice of a mother at home.

Why did that sacrifice seem to us such a great one?

Martine, my wife, grew up in rural Ohio in the late 1950s and 1960s. Her family included three children, two parents, and a grandmother. Her mother worked at a job outside the home—a somewhat unusual situation in those days—and Martine keenly felt her mother's absence. Not so much for the big things, but for the little things—the little back-and-forth conversations that happen spontaneously between a mother and her daughter, the little matter of sharing a laugh or merely sharing a silence. These little things can add up, creating a dimension of relationship that can only come from time spent together. Of course, Martine and her mother had what has come to be called "quality time." But quality time is only for big things.

There was time to talk about big things. There was time in the evenings, when her mother came home, tired from work, and on weekends, when there were errands to run, shopping to do, and household chores to handle. But sometimes she wanted to see her mother in the morning or the afternoon, or to find her home when she came home from school, and of course she couldn't.

Martine was studious. That was countercultural in this rural Ohio town. The weekly high school football games were the school's main focus—in fact, the main source of community pride. Few students or parents cared much about academics, and the school did little to encourage or support the rare students who might be thinking of college. She succeeded despite her school, not because of it, learning early that what mattered in education was not what an institution did or did not offer, but personal relationships, personal attention, and personal effort. Luckily, her seventh-grade history teacher recognized her academic potential, and even more luckily, he became principal of the high school. He stepped outside of the institutional definition of the role of principal to provide personal feedback, guidance, and latitude for Martine to excel. A math teacher also took a personal interest, encouraging her to work ahead in the textbook and offering extra tutoring for the material she tackled outside the classes.

Personal relationships therefore allowed her to excel academically despite the weak school. She was lucky to have met a few teachers who did have a strong personal commitment to students. Yet she can count those teachers on one hand, and the help they provided was usually after school hours. It wasn't the institution but stepping outside the institution that contributed most to her education. Maybe we remember such outstanding teachers, in fact, because they are so rare. Their rarity is what makes them memorable and precious. Maybe, too, the constraints of the institution help ensure that such teachers will be rare.[3]

For my part, I grew up in East St. Louis, Illinois, a place whose whole history recorded the failure of institutions, governments, and structures. My father's family of Sullivans and O'Neills and Goldons had lived in that town since the nineteenth century. My great-grandparents owned a tavern on Bloody Island, which had risen up in the middle of the Mississippi River a few years before the 1811 earthquake on the New Madrid Fault. Being outside the jurisdiction of either Illinois or Missouri, the new island gained popularity as a site for duels of honor, bare-knuckle boxing, and cockfights. In 1837, the young Robert E. Lee built a dam that diverted the river and attached the island to what was then called Illinois Town. The town's reputation for violence and catastrophe got so bad that in order to change its image, the city fathers changed its name, and it became East St. Louis. They didn't change the violence, though.

My father's Irish mother married an immigrant from England who brought the name Millman with him. Beyond the name, we don't know much about him, or about his family in England, because he died when my father was three years old. An engineer on a boat that was probably dredging the Mississippi River, he had to climb a mast of some sort to make repairs during a storm, and lightning struck him, so he fell to the deck, where broken ribs punctured his lungs. My father grew up fatherless. Eventually, his mother married a man who proved to be a good stepfather, but my father was already twelve by then, and when he had needed a father there was none. After serving in the Army Air Force during World War II, he graduated from college, married, and worked in accounting. He started studying for his CPA, but reconsidered, weighing the opportunity for a much higher income against the time that it would take from his family. Family would always come before work, or money, or anything else. He measured success by the time he spent with his family.

Of course, this meant financial sacrifices. His mother had inherited from her sister a house in East St. Louis—by the postwar years, the family had mostly left that hard town behind—and my father bought it. When I was very young, he showed me the upper rooms where his aunt had sheltered "a colored family" from the violence of 1917, when local employers had hired "Negroes" to replace striking Irish and the city had exploded in a rage of shooting and lynching. By the time I was born, East St. Louis was on its way to becoming almost completely African-American. When my father played catch with my brother and me in the yard, fatherless boys from the neighborhood would come to hang on our fence and watch. My father always waved them in, and took time to play catch with each of them. He remembered what it had been like to watch other boys playing catch with their fathers and having no father. We lived in the house until the late 1960s. Then, rhetoric of the "kill Whitey" sort became common, and snipers picked off the old white man who had the house with a pear tree at one end of the block, and a bomb exploded at the other end of the block. It would simply have been foolish to stay any longer.

I had spent a lot of my recess time playing the dozens with

classmates at the local Catholic parochial school. That parochial school was probably better than the local public school. But in high school, where most students had come from better elementary schools, I found that in subjects like math, teachers expected more preparation than I'd gotten. Students who had attended elementary schools in better neighborhoods were far ahead of me on the first day of my freshman year in high school.

What happened to my daughter brought back memories of my own grade school, where I usually got poor marks on the "respects authority" line of my report card. All things considered, it was not hard to decide that homeschooling would have little downside for us. When the only alternative is a poor school, homeschooling has no educational opportunity cost. It's not as though, by homeschooling, we would be depriving our children of something better. There would be no financial opportunity cost, either. Martine was already staying at home with our children, so our family would not incur an income loss by homeschooling.

Setting Out

Still, the prospect of homeschooling frightened us. Homeschooling was not entirely unknown when we started, in 1993, but it had a reputation as a lifestyle choice for communal hippies, separatist Christians, paranoid libertarians, and other fringe crazies inhabiting either the extreme left or

Hard Economics and the Homeschool Choice

Our state's "best" school districts have high house prices and high taxes. With only one income, we couldn't afford to live in those neighborhoods. In fact, those neighborhoods are unaffordable to most of the state's population. Median housing prices in our state's "best" school districts are double or triple the median home prices for the state as a whole. Unsurprisingly, the people in those houses have median household incomes that are double or triple the statewide median, and census data indicate that over three-quarters of such affluent households have two incomes.

Those who prefer private elementary schools can easily expect to pay tuition and fees reaching toward the five figures. Tuitions at the best college prep schools are now in the $20,000 to $30,000 range.

The choice to raise a family on one income put the best public and private school educations out of reach for us, as it does for most. Yet homeschooling allowed us to secure for our children an education at least equal to, and often even better than, what is available in the pricier school districts of our state.

the extreme right of the sociopolitical spectrum. We knew only one other homeschooling family, a girl from Martine's rural Ohio high school class. She was a strongly evangelical Christian who had married a schoolteacher and was raising, in addition to her own children, a series of foster kids on a farm hundreds of miles from us. Nothing we knew about her suggested we might have anything in common except whatever she and Martine remembered from high school, such as playing poker during chemistry lab.

We swallowed hard and told ourselves that we would be on our own, but that we could do worse than fail—we could refuse to try.

We told the school that we expected to be traveling extensively during the coming year—which was true—and wanted the children to accompany us so that they would have a chance to see the country, visit historic sites, and so on. We asked the school what the children would need to study in order to keep pace with the school curriculum. The school refused to share any information about curriculum. So we contacted our local public school and found that the curriculum standards were matters of public record. We got a copy and, scanning the materials to be covered at each grade level, saw how little mystery there was about them.

The Internet was in its infancy in 1993, but by plugging away on CompuServe and asking friends for leads and digging through articles at the library we learned about a Catholic homeschooling conference scheduled to meet in Manassas, Virginia. The National Association of Catholic Home Educators (NACHE), founded just a year before, was holding a convention that summer, so we decided to drive down and check it out. We took all the kids, of course, and while Martine attended talks and breakout sessions, the rest of us toured the site of the first and second battles of Manassas. Using travel as a homeschooling opportunity, and home-schooling as a travel opportunity, would later become part of our standard MO.

In the curriculum fair adjoining that conference hall, some vendors sold *The Latin Mass* magazines and reprinted 1950s textbooks. Some people were paying thousands of dollars to curriculum providers in order to base their home-schooling on what seemed to us the same drudgework and authoritarianism that we were trying to help our children escape. Nevertheless, something revolutionary was going on here. In fact, even the reactionaries were advancing the revolution by their determination to break away from the Catholic-school bureaucracy. By looking at education as their own responsibility, instead of leaving it to Father or Sister, they were flexing muscles that the pre–Vatican II Catholic laity never knew it had. There was a radical energy in the air, the kind that blows apart stereotypes and leaves you wondering how to describe what is going on. As speakers famous for their conservatism, such as Father John Hardon, a spiritual adviser to Mother Teresa, called for the laity to shrug off the strictures of clerical authoritarianism and take the job of education back, they seemed anything but conservative.

We came back from Manassas convinced not only that we could homeschool but also that under the circumstances nothing else made any sense at all for us. We had met some homeschooling families at the conference, and they didn't seem all that different from us. Although some homeschoolers had master's degrees or Ph.Ds, most didn't, and in any case it didn't matter—there was and to this day is no evidence whatsoever that a mother's expertise in a subject determines her success as a homeschooler.[4]

For that matter, students in public and private schools often enough have teachers whose expertise in the subject is questionable. With respect to the public schools, the authors of *The Shopping Mall High School* wrote, "Additional math courses are taught by physical education teachers who have seniority over new candidates trained in mathematics. New courses in physics and chemistry are being staffed from the long-standing surplus of biology teachers, many of whom never took a college course in chemistry or physics."[5] Catholic schools traditionally assigned teachers to teach subjects in which they had little or no formal training but merely stayed a chapter or two ahead of the children in the textbooks.[6]

Martine thought that she, too, ought to be able to stay at least a chapter or two ahead of her children in the textbooks. Perhaps she could do even more. What we didn't yet have, though, were textbooks. At first, she thought she needed them—but the vendors at this conference were selling what she would call "Catholic school in a can," sométimes complete with scripts telling mothers precisely what they should say (to their own children!) in the course of a class. She continued to research options through the summer, and eventually discovered a company that offered a catalog of textbooks, guidance on developing lesson plans, and basic hand-holding. After reviewing the catalog, she opted to buy a few work-

books in writing and math, but she put the rest of the curriculum together herself. With exceptions so rare that it is
hard to remember one, textbooks leach the interest and color
out of almost any subjects; textbooks are to books as pow-
dered food supplements are to a good, balanced meal. Thus,
the reading curriculum for our second- and first-grade girls
started out with the Little House series of novel-memoirs relating the adventures of a girl and her family on the American
frontier. Frequent trips to the library supplemented this series with books on history and science and anything else that
caught the children's attention. We also traveled. Free from
the school schedule, we took our first long homeschooling
road trip in September, just as school would have been getting under way.

I had contracted to write a book about the recent wrenching dislocations in the international financial system as
power shifted from governments to private traders. So we decided to drive up to New Hampshire and experience something of the milieu that John Maynard Keynes and others
were in at the end of World War II as they negotiated the
agreements that created the postwar financial order.

After we got back from the trip, we settled into a routine
of homeschooling. Lest the word "routine" give a false impression, we were not the kind of homeschooling family that
mounts a blackboard in the corner, rings a bell, and has class
at set hours every day. Many homeschooling books and
guides emphasize the routine and the structure of the homeschooling exercise. We experimented with several approaches

over time. We found that it is not so much the structure but the context of structure, not so much the lines but the white space between and around the lines that really matters in our own pedagogy.

CHAPTER ONE TAKEAWAYS

- ✓ One of the most important decisions we made on the road to homeschooling was that our children should have a very costly "luxury": a full-time mom.

- ✓ Homeschooling makes it possible to give a child an excellent education without incurring heavy debt to purchase a house in a "good" neighborhood with "good" schools.

- ✓ Homeschooling can provide an education superior to that available even in schools that are considered good.

- ✓ There was and to this day is no evidence whatsoever that a mother's or father's expertise in a subject determines success as a homeschooler.

TWO

Looking out the Window as Homeschooling

On a crisp February day, we're having some trees cut down in the front yard; they're blocking sun from the solar array we just installed on the roof. Our sons are sitting at the window and watching. They notice how the tree guys act when they get out of the truck, and see that there is a kind of hierarchy. There's the boss, whose name is on the truck. There are a couple of white hotshots with wraparound sunglasses. They start tossing weighted lines up into the trees to find sound branches, and when they find a sound one, use it to anchor a climbing rope. A few Hispanics do the heavy, dirty work, clearing out the fallen stuff, chopping the weedy undergrowth, and feeding the chipper. When the branch cutting starts, the boys notice that everyone stands or walks around the perimeter of an unmarked safety zone, seeming to know where the branches will fall. The perimeter moves depending on what branches the climber is cutting. Martine uses the occasion to raise questions—she doesn't ask them so much as encourage the boys to ask them. They answer one another's questions, disagree, discuss. It's a fascinating show. I have trouble pulling myself away from it to go back to my desk and get to work again. It's a teachable moment.

Our approach to homeschooling is improvisational. It makes use of the moment at hand, the present moment, the only moment in which you can find a teachable moment. This is probably impossible in the context of a school—literally impossible. Different children are ready for different things at different moments. You can't follow a standard curriculum with standard timetables and expect, except by lucky coincidence, to address the object of a child's curiosity at the moment when the object becomes interesting to the child. So schools let a lot of teachable moments go by, simply because their rules and constraints don't allow much deviation.

The schools we knew were like oompah bands—the same tune, the same rhythm, over and over, child after child, class after class. Our homeschooling approach is more like jazz. We have a set of objectives that we hope to hit in a year or so, certain skills or material that we do want the children to address. But we're flexible about how we achieve that goal and we're flexible about when we achieve it. We improvise along the way.

The children help shape the set with their own rhythms and riffs, and we play off them, with them, sometimes against them. Billy was sitting at the dinner table one night, finishing a word list he'd put together, words he'd come across reading Agatha Christie novels, words he wanted to remember and use. He had also lately gotten interested in history. So mystery and history became a big part of his curriculum. He would make connections between what he read about in early American history and what he heard on the radio, and notice that history is full of mystery. What did Polk's fiction of a Mexican attack on American soil have in common with the fictitious attack on an American vessel in the Gulf of Tonkin under LBJ, and the allegations that Saddam Hussein was hiding weapons of mass destruction in Iraq?

When the children raise that kind of question, we explore it. We follow the trail where it leads. We don't have to say, "Don't you have math homework to do?" or "We'll get to that next year when we study contemporary history. Now we're studying the American Revolution." We might even put math and history and English and everything else aside for a while to do something else whose importance is more immediate— such as looking out the window at something happening that won't happen again.

The power saws are running, and branches are falling. Lead-weighted lines are darting up over branches and arcing down. A lithe man with a power saw dangling from his belt is swinging from the top of a tree, smoking a cigarette. Mom says that it's risky. Blaise says, "He likes risk!" The seed is planted for some future discussion of financial economics, and how different risk appetites lead people to make different kinds of decisions. We won't have that conversation now.

But in a year or two or three, when the subject comes up, someone will mention the time we had the trees cut down to open the canopy for sun to hit the solar array.

The line draws a parabola briefly in the air as the weight takes it over the branch—there's a lesson in geometry. Principles of physics may help us explain why the workers can safely stand there but not a few feet to either side, and having seen them moving along, knowing this, will help when we come to study that subject. The crew segregates itself for lunch, the browns keeping to themselves, the whites keeping to themselves. In that we have matter for the study of history, sociology, economics, and more. All in due time.

Could a school system possibly improvise this way? It probably would be the death of school as America knows it. The fact is, our approach to education is radically different from that of the educational system. By radical, I mean at the root. We have a different idea of what education means, a different understanding of its purpose and process. We weren't completely clear about what we thought when we began, but we were already acting on it. The longer we have homeschooled, the clearer it has become that we and the school system use the same word, "education," to mean different things.

American schools have, since the late nineteenth century, demanded various things of children, but never that they become subjects responsible for seeking truth. Instead, children have always been objects of one process or another, and they continue to be. As the educational historian Herbert Kliebard says, "Work right now is clearly the dominant purpose of education. There's almost no stress on learning literature or music or art or languages. It's an indication of the success of the movement to transform the purpose of education. You don't hear anybody say anymore, 'I'm going to school to become well educated,' or even 'to appreciate fine literature'. That's old-fashioned and gone by the boards."[1]

Kliebard's great work, *The Struggle for the American Curriculum: 1893–1958,* shows that since the very inception of mass public schooling, control of our schools and curriculum has been the prize in a sort of open contest among various pressure groups and ideologies. The groups and ideologies change but the contest continues. Educational standards and the content of the curriculum are political trophies. Since political struggles and compromises have been shaping our schools for so long, it's no wonder that schools do not look or act as if they were instruments built to achieve a clear educational purpose or objective. Viewed from our homeschooling perspective, they look as if they were trying to balance several different and unrelated or even contradictory purposes or objectives. It would surprise us if they were to do a good job achieving any one of these purposes or objectives.

Educational scholars and historians note that confusion and controversy over the job of schools seems to be the norm in American schools. Patricia Albjerg Graham, former director of the National Institute of Education and Charles Warren Research Professor of the History of American Education at Harvard, writes of a varying drumbeat to which American society has demanded that schoolchildren march:

Sometimes it wanted children to solve the social problems, such as racial segregation, adults could not handle. Sometimes it tacitly supported some schools as warehouses, not instructional facilities. Sometimes it sought schooling to be the equalizer in a society in which the gap between the rich and the poor was growing. . . . Now, the drumbeat demands that all children achieve academically at a high level and the measure of that achievement is tests.[2]

The decision to send a child to school is a decision to send a child into an environment with an organization and culture shaped by such seldom articulated assumptions and compromises. It is a decision to entrust a child to an enterprise whose tacit missions and goals may be different from the ones written on the wall. These missions and goals are both political and economic.

Today, the political pressure comes to bear over whether schools should teach evolution or intelligent design; offer prayer or sex education in the classroom; present literature as written or use versions rewritten to advance a contemporary social agenda; and so on. This contest does not really aim to teach children how to find truth. It is about who will have the power to indoctrinate them. So the contest is not just about what to teach. It is also about who wins. It is a political struggle that treats a child's education as a political trophy. As the sociologist Joseph Crosfield has written, "Psychologists may show that the Pledge of Allegiance every morning has no discernible effect upon patriotic feeling, but this is not the issue as status elements are involved. What such curricular changes 'bear witness' to is the domination of one cultural group and the subordination of another. As most educators know, schools are run for adults, not children."[3]

Misguided Trust

We hadn't been thinking about all that when we sent our own children to school. Since we had gone to school ourselves, we sent our children to school not because we'd thought the matter through but just because that's what you did. That was what everyone did, wasn't it? Some other mothers, friends of Martine, had enrolled their children in a preschool and we followed them, enrolling Bridget in a preschool. The next step was kindergarten, and then elementary school. It was easy to keep moving along the line. It didn't take any thought at all. The only question we asked was "which school," not "whether school."

But that was a real abrogation of our parental responsibility and, viewed from our present vantage point, it is shocking and shaming. How could we do such a thing? How could we assume that schools could be trusted? We knew that most institutions couldn't be. We had experienced the vicissitudes of an economy so unstable that it left us too jaded to get a thrill out of roller coasters. (Even the big Nitro at Six Flags is a yawn after you've experienced downsizing in action.) We lived in New Jersey, where thousands of people who had relied on explicit and implicit promises from employers had been left holding the bag.

We had written about business and finance and understood such concepts as agency risk—the notion that the people who manage an organization tend to manage it in their own interest, not the interest of shareholders or other stakeholders. There was absolutely no reason to suppose that the educational system was any different, whether Catholic or public. Yet we made our educational decisions as if we really believed that the educational system was different. Despite the evidence, we trusted.

This is especially perplexing, in retrospect. Even as children, we had discovered the fallibility of conventional wisdom and the great risks involved in trusting experts and institutions to do what is best. Martine had seen what an expert did to her father. She was just entering her teens when a physician at a hospital treating her father for cancer blundered, gave him too much radiation, and turned him into a semi-invalid for the remaining decade of his life. Although the doctor's flub left the family financially strapped, and with continuing medical expenses, those were what the profession must now look on as the halcyon days—before malpractice suits became commonplace.

We had this kind of vision in common. I never saw any reason to trust government's promise of public service, because the institutions I knew so clearly served private interests, the interests of those who held the jobs and controlled the money. Growing up in East St. Louis, I got my hair cut by a barber named Charlie who voted early and often, as the saying goes, under more names than Charlie, led to the polls by the ward boss who lived a few doors down from us and who presumably made the effort worth Charlie's while. As far as the great public itself was concerned, family stories of riots in the early years of the century, and my own familiarity with racial violence during the riotous sixties, did not lead me to faith in the *vox populi,* either.

Our skepticism about conventional received wisdom served us reasonably well in our career choices. After college, we both went to work in journalism. We quickly learned that the truth was flexible when editors were in the mood to bend it to please advertisers, readers, owners, or themselves. Perhaps our personal and professional experiences disposed us to cock an eyebrow a bit more readily and a bit more archly at public opinion and what we read in the papers. The stronger the polls seemed in support of any point of view, the more apt we were to remember that public opinion is usually a product of careful and costly engineering. We more or less took it for granted that the official and generally accepted version of anything is at best a half-truth, and often enough a lie. We generally tested anything we heard or read against our own experience and our own reasoning. We had defied conventional wisdom by deciding that we would live on one income in order to provide the children with a full-time mother. Yet despite all this, we had sent our children to school. Why?

We've wondered about this with homeschooling friends who, like us, had suspended their critical judgment when they put their children in schools, only to recover it later. Most of them, like us, are one-income, mom-at-home families that turned to homeschooling after discovering how far schools fell short. For example, there's the family whose mother had been a Ph.D. candidate in French literature at Yale and whose father worked as an engineer at AT&T. Like us, they were urban pioneers on a rough frontier. She decided to stay home when her first child was born, and after experiencing the decline of the local public schools, ended up homeschooling her two girls. Yet out of a sense of civic obligation, she volunteered her time to support (and try to slow the deterioration of) the same local public schools. But there's also the family whose mother was working as a researcher at a pharmaceutical company, and opted to stay home because of the toll that work-related travel was taking on her family. Her husband started his own business after a merger took his job, and their family lives in a middle-class suburb, with reasonably good middle-class schools. They opted for homeschooling after the local public school principal told them frankly that the public school could not provide the kind of educational enrichment their precocious son needed if he were to be challenged.

A school doesn't have to be in a ghetto to be inadequate. Even supposedly good schools have limitations that prevent them from providing the kind of education that homeschooling offers.

Value investors, such as Warren Buffett, get rich by looking carefully at many companies and then choosing to buy those stocks that are real bargains because they are selling for less than the companies issuing them are worth. The stock prices are low not because there is something wrong with the companies but because other investors in the market haven't done the same homework as the value investors, and therefore haven't recognized the value. Homeschoolers are something like value investors in that they look very carefully at the educational choices available to them and choose the one that offers the most value.

Relatively few people seem to analyze their educational investments as thoroughly as they might analyze a stock investment.

The *New York Times* has reported the plight of people who moved from New York City to New York's affluent suburbs, bought expensive houses, and paid high taxes for the schools, only to be "disappointed by classes that were too crowded, bare-bones arts and sports programs, and an emphasis on standardized testing rather than creative teaching."[4]

By Any Measure

The research on homeschooling is unambiguous: even when measured by such conventional yardsticks as standardized tests, homeschooling delivers a better educational return than conventional schools. The most extensive study so far occurred in 1998, when Lawrence Rudner, then director of the ERIC Clearinghouse on Assessment and Evaluation, College of Library and Information Services, University of Maryland, College Park, surveyed 20,760 homeschooled students from over 11,930 families. Depending on grade level, the students had taken one of two standardized tests, either

(continued)

the Iowa Tests of Basic Skills (ITBS) or the Tests of Achievement and Proficiency (TAP).

Dr. Rudner found that homeschoolers in his sample typically scored in the 70th or 80th percentile, far above public, Catholic, or private school students. They performed one grade level above their age-level peers through grade four, and opened an even wider gap above grade five. "Students who have been homeschooled their entire academic life have higher scholastic achievement test scores than students who have also attended other educational programs," Rudner wrote. "There are no meaningful differences in achievement by gender, whether the student is enrolled in a full-service curriculum, or whether a parent holds a state issued teaching certificate."[5]

Other researchers have reported that the homeschooled participate in more extracurricular activities,[6] and enjoy a more diverse range of social contacts,[7] and higher scores on socialization, social maturity, living skills, and communications tests than schoolchildren. "The results were striking— the mean problem behavior score for children attending conventional schools was more than eight times higher than that of the homeschooled group,"[8] one researcher observed. That's not to say that no one anywhere can find a school that is as good as or better than homeschooling, but when we talk broadly about educational choices we talk in terms of the statistical "law of large numbers." Other alternatives to conventional public schools, such as charter schools, seem to have succeeded, but the evidence of their superiority is not nearly as clear as it is for homeschooling. For example, a study conducted in 2003 by the RAND Corporation examined charter schools in California and concluded, "Overall, the analysis shows that charter school students are keeping pace with comparable students in conventional public schools."[9] Merely "keeping pace"!

G-Men in Suits

It took a lot to break us out of our complacent comfort with the conventional path to and through schools. It took a lot to activate our skepticism. The conversation with the principal, as blunt and clear as it was, might not have been enough to convince us to homeschool if it hadn't been for another, almost simultaneous message that we should temper with a dose of skepticism our trust in experts and institutions.

We had our meeting with the principal in February, a while after an incident that would be fundamental to our children's education in civics. They happened to have been home because a teachers' meeting had closed the school for the day. We were getting lunch on the table and the children were playing in the living room when the doorbell rang. Bridget called out that someone was at the door. Martine took a look and said, "Greg, they're either used-car salesmen or they're with the government." Why she should think of used-car salesmen, I don't know. We bought used cars, of course, but not from door-to-door salesmen. It was probably something about the credibility and the trust these visitors inspired at first glance. They were white, wearing suits and spit-shined shoes, and they were in our neighborhood, which is to say, out of place.

White people were uncommon in our neighborhood. These two were tall and politely menacing. They identified themselves as Secret Service and asked to come in. I looked at their ID and opened the door. They walked across the porch, briefly perplexed by a pile of green tomatoes we had salvaged from an early frost and destined for salsa and mincemeat. The four children crowded around as the agents relaxed into chairs in the living room, accepted an offer of coffee, and started their version of small talk. Martine sent the children upstairs to watch *Fantasia*. Then the agents said that they had come about a story I had written for a small financial magazine.

The story was about an interpretation of tax law that had given a break to some corporations. This was one of those obscure, arcane, technical, legalistic issues on which billions of dollars can go one way or another. Fortunately for the corporations, it would be going their way. Most people didn't know and wouldn't care about it. The only thing that made the Secret Service take an interest was the fact that the story named the corporations involved and the money the break had saved them. This was, allegedly, confidential tax information and it was, allegedly, a crime to write about it. The Secret Service was involved because it is part of the Treasury Department, as is the Internal Revenue Service. These agents were investigating a leak. They wanted to know who had provided the information.

I explained that I couldn't tell them. They explained that they would be willing to send me to jail if I did not cooperate.

We smiled at each other for a moment, and then one of the agents suggested that we might have been forgetful on our tax returns. This was hard for him to do with a straight face, given the pile of green tomatoes on the porch and the furnishings in our home. But he did his best. Spotting a rug with an Oriental pattern, he observed that it looked to be a high-quality piece of carpet, and asked where we'd bought it. When Martine told him we'd bought it at Caldor, a now bankrupt discount retailer, he raised his eyebrows, nodded skeptically, rubbed the rug to feel the pile, nodded again in the manner of a real connoisseur, lifted the corner, and exposed the big red "Clearance" tag still on the bottom. He dropped it, and we smiled at each other again.

I excused myself for a moment and called my editor, who put me in touch with the magazine's attorney, and at the mention of an attorney the agents made a prompt and polite exit. I was surprised at how quickly it was all over. I didn't know that they were going to the phone company to subpoena all my telephone records, and then all the records of anyone I had phoned who seemed to them to be worth investigating, all in order to reconstruct the chain of contacts that might lead them to my source. There were supposed to be legal and constitutional protections against this kind of thing, but when we went to court to fight those subpoenas we found out that those protections were not much protection at all. The story became a minor cause célèbre in journalistic circles,[10] and around the time we were deciding to leave the school, congressional hearings were scheduled.

A Lesson in Civics

Over the objections of her second-grade teacher, who opposed her taking a day off from class to travel to Washington and see a congressional hearing, Bridget came with me. Civics is the class where children learn how government works, and she learned about how her government worked by listening to people tell how federal agents had put their telephone habits under surveillance, gotten their phone records, and studied the calls they had made, all with no warrants and no review by any court, and merely because they had at some point talked with her father on the telephone. She learned a lesson about the Bill of Rights, about the First Amendment, which guarantees our freedom of the press, and about the Fourth Amendment, which protects us against unreasonable search and seizure. It was an important lesson in civics and I'm proud to say that she has never forgotten it.

We didn't yet understand but we were beginning to feel that everything that happens in life can be part of a child's education, as long as the child pays attention and asks such questions as "why" and "how," and the teacher helps point the way to the answers. Martine and I had attended schools, so we had taken the annoyances and deficiencies of schools for granted, the way you take mosquitoes for granted on a summer evening. Among the most annoying was the general tendency of schools to discourage such questions.

Bridget had a habit of asking these questions even about

the premises of arithmetic problems, as we noticed when we tried to help her with her homework. If the problem began, "John has two oranges and three apples, and wants to share them with two friends," then she wanted to know, "Are they good friends or just acquaintances? Why is John carrying so much fruit? Why does he just have two oranges, but three apples? How come his friends don't have any fruit? If John has so much and they have none, why doesn't John just let his friends have an orange and an apple apiece? Wouldn't that be polite? If John's still hungry he could probably get another orange where he got the first two, couldn't he?"

None of these questions has anything to do with arithmetic, but as far as Bridget was concerned, the arithmetic wasn't really as important as these questions. And in a way she was right. They do seem to be questions as reasonable to ask about the situation as the question of how to divvy up the fruit. In fact, the issues addressed by her questions may be more important than arithmetic in the long run. Bridget's focus on the periphery of the immediate arithmetical problem was hard to appreciate when it meant she took hours to do homework that should have taken minutes. It sometimes did exhaust our patience. Yet it also showed us something important about where her interests lay and how her mind worked. Math turned out not to be Bridget's strong suit, but a decade after she began to ask such questions she chose to major in philosophy and international development, got active in student government, and became a seasoned debater at the college level.

Questions that are peripheral to the problem at hand may be central to a child's development. One of the great advantages of homeschooling is that it allows a parent to develop a curriculum tailored to the child instead of tailoring the child to the curriculum. Schools probably can't do this. They operate on schedules that require teachers to cover certain material in certain periods of time in order to prepare students for high-stakes tests. If a teacher let one student interrupt the math lesson with a question about distributive justice, there might be another question from another student about why apples and pears are different, and from another about whether dinosaurs ate apples, and—who knows?—one of the children might even ask why apples fall out of trees but never fall up from the ground. Each question could open into a fascinating scientific inquiry. In fact, one prominent scientific author recently discussed the last of them at length in an excellent popular introduction to contemporary physics.[11] Curiosity about such questions is the energy that powers education in the long run, but schools waste most of that energy. They are like factories whose production process wastes energy. Homeschooling is like a factory whose cogeneration plant captures that energy to make electricity.

So the question we ask, knowing what we know now, is: How could we ever have sent our children to school? We've learned a lot since the time we went to the public school to get a copy of the curriculum standards. At the time, it seemed natural to suppose that homeschooling meant teaching at home the material that children would otherwise learn in school. We knew that the schools available to us were inadequate, but we implicitly assumed that the institution of schooling was good. This seems to be the same assumption that others have long made, if the annual Phi Delta Kappa/ Gallup Poll of the Public's Attitudes Toward the Public Schools is any indication. In 2005 and 2006, this poll showed that fewer than half of Americans believe that the schools in their communities deserve A or B grades for performance. Even among parents whose children attend public schools, only a little over half believe that the public schools in their communities are very good. Yet they seem to think that the public school system is the best source of solutions for its own problems.[12]

We disagree. The problem, as we see it, is that the school curriculum and school methodology are not about education as we see education. Even before the No Child Left Behind program narrowed the focus of classroom instruction, the school curriculum and school methodology were products of a political and ideological struggle that went now one way, now another. For us, education means a kind of growth and development that seems to have no constituency within the school system. When we say "education," we mean a process of growing in truth and freedom. We couldn't find this kind of education by looking in the classroom. We had to look out the window.

CHAPER TWO TAKEAWAYS

✓ Everything that happens in life can be part of a child's education, as long as the child pays attention and asks such questions as "why" and "how" and someone is paying enough attention to help the child find the answer.

✓ Questions that are peripheral to the problem at hand may be central to a child's development.

✓ A school-like curriculum and school-like pedagogy only make sense in the context of a school.

✓ Homeschooling allows children to learn by looking out the window.

THREE

Our Three R's:
Rhetoric, Rhythm, and Randori

When he was ten, Joey, our second son, got a tool kit for Christmas. The next day he took apart an old clock radio and came to me with a round black component that looked like the speaker. "Look, Dad, it's a magnet!" He brought a screw close enough for the magnet to pull it out of his hand; the screw jumped through the air and stuck tight. Then he showed me how it felt when the magnet tugged a screwdriver. "Why do they put a magnet in a radio?" he asked. I told him it would be interesting to find out, so we started investigating.

Joey took things apart for weeks: old radios, old clocks, anything that caught his eye. Fortunately, he asked first. I don't recall exactly when or how the bug bit him. It worked out well, though. I hadn't realized how many old, broken electronics items we had accumulated, and disposing of these things isn't as simple as putting them in a trash bag and setting them in the garbage can. It takes some forethought to plan a special errand to a dump or recycling station, so the job goes on my "when I have time for a special errand" list. Something else always seems more important, so our basement has more junk in it than a well-managed basement should. Now that Joey has turned the junk into a pedagogical treasure trove, I feel a lot better about not having thrown it out. Random disassembly of electronic devices isn't a scheduled activity on any school agenda that I know of and wasn't initially part of our homeschooling regimen, but it is now, at least for Joey. Who knows where it might lead?

Taking things apart is just the flip side of building them. Seeing how things come apart shows you how they fit together. The children built (from kits) their loft beds and the file cabinets and bookshelves in the "schoolroom." Building involves reading directions carefully, proceeding logically, and understanding spatial relationships, and on the whole is an excellent form of education. But we don't plan ahead for a curriculum in building. When the need comes up and the job has to be done, someone does it and learns from it. Similarly, when a discarded radio catches a child's eye, there's an opportunity for learning. We rely on randomness. There is a kind of blessing in spontaneity. Jazz plays in the background.

Not all homeschoolers think this way. One friend of ours speaks with firm conviction of homeschooling as a "profession." Her household is a model of order and discipline. The thought of disorder as something to be tolerated, much less celebrated, would shock her. But even she puts all her plans and routines aside to respond to an urgent demand in the present moment. She spoke with us about a serious "character issue" with one of her children, a problem with temper, that took "half my time and energy" for a long stretch of months. It was a serious and unexpected disruption to her schedule. "But I knew that the most important thing was to address character," she says, "and everything else would come in time."[1]

The person is the priority—not the schedule, not the agenda, not anything else. Education is about the development of the child, the whole person of the child, not just the mind (and certainly not the school's average performance on some standardized test). So our approach is not to assign work, look to see that it's done, and move on to the next assignment. It isn't the strict approach of saying, "Go do your math!" and they go off and do forty math problems and that's it. This isn't our approach, because what matters is not getting the child to produce work but, rather, getting the child to become a fully free and actualized human being.

We want the child to master the math concept, but more important we want the child to experience the joy of discovery in mathematics, the thrill of victory that comes only with concentrated intellectual effort and achievement. We don't want the process to be clouded by a power struggle, but we do want the child to have the security of knowing that someone is in charge. The ideal is that the child will find the joy and choose to do the work. Failing that, we will enforce drill until mastery.

Too often, children in schools produce work for the wrong

reasons, for dehumanizing reasons—for example, because they are afraid not to.[2] Fear is not a very effective motivator, as almost any good manager knows. Fear can only elicit compliance. It may get short-term results, but it exacts a steep long-term cost in morale and spirit. Motivation and commitment do not come from fear but from trust. That said, we have sometimes succumbed to the temptation to use threats and punishments, and in the hoary tradition of parents we have painted a dark picture of the hard life of toilet scrubbing that those who don't do their homework can expect. But we try not to do this and we see it as a failure on our part when we do.

Our real aim is to help the children consistently choose what they should choose. There are two reasons why they might not choose rightly. On the one hand, they might not recognize what is good about doing something they'd rather not do. A lot of things might seem more appealing than math homework. If this is the case, the problem is one of perspective, and our job is to help them see the advantages of doing what they should do. But sometimes they do see the advantages, yet just can't seem to reach for them. The problem isn't that they don't want to do the right thing but that their bodies won't let them focus. In fact, more often than not, this is the problem.

So a third to a half of homeschooling time may consist of helping a child learn to settle down and do the work. Martine was interested to see, on a news show about autism, a hugging machine someone had developed to help calm autistic children. None of our children is autistic, but when it is hard to settle down, a hug helps them. There's something about the physical contact, the reassurance of being held. She used to hold the young ones on her lap when they started writing Chinese characters and sometimes sat with her arm around an older child struggling with particularly challenging math. This comforts and encourages them, and once they have the comfort and encouragement, they seem to be able to break through and continue on their own. They can make the right choices then.

The Soft Way: Lessons from Judo

We do not operate on a strict timetable, because a strict time-table would not allow for these expected yet not predictable needs. We do set daily, weekly, monthly, annual, even lifetime goals, but the timetable has to be flexible so that we can re-spond to the demands of the present moment. For example, we had planned to get an early start on high school work while Bridget was in the eighth grade, but we happened to move to another house that year. We had long outgrown our old one and had postponed moving until it could no longer be put off. We would have stayed in Plainfield, but fashion had discovered the bigger houses there, many of which were beautiful old Victorians, and the combination of prices and taxes put them out of our financial comfort zone.

We shopped intensively for almost two years, during an-other housing market bubble. Given the nature of our work, we could have moved anywhere in the country, but we wanted to stay within reasonable commuting distance of our dojo and other activities that were important for the children. The children were, of course, part of the house-hunting process, the older ones even learning something about house prices and mortgages. Eventually, we found a house about fifteen minutes west of where we were living. Apparently it had started as a hunting cabin, but a succession of owners had expanded it. In a market that was hot for colonials and cathedral ceilings, this was an unfashionable brick ranch, midway up a steep hill, more or less in the woods. Because of land-use regulations, the woods would remain woods. There were no near neighbors, and except for traffic noise during the rush hours, the only sound was birdsong. The water supply was from a good well, and the roof had southern exposure— perfect, we would later discover, for solar panels. The price was within our range, and taxes were comparable to what we had been paying on our old house. The house had lingered unsold for months, so we had some negotiating flexibility. We bought it.

After we closed on the new house and were getting ready to list the old one, Bridget dislocated a shoulder doing randori (free-style sparring judo practice). Her injury put both the move and the schoolwork behind schedule. We all rolled with it, though, and eventually came up on our feet. We sold the old house without a real estate agent, to friends of friends, who let us take six months to get everything moved.

We often draw on lessons from judo and apply them throughout our curriculum. One of the most important things to remember about homeschooling, as about judo, is to roll when you fall. An acquaintance whose family tried homeschooling for a while showed us how important that is. He was quite rigid about schedules and timetables. When he found out that we had not started "doing school" by November (the year we moved), he let us know how much he disapproved. He would have been even more surprised by how seldom we really "did school."

Both our own experience and our acquaintance with many homeschooling families have taught us that the people most apt to continue homeschooling have a high degree of flexibility and a willingness to roll with the throws. Because we could adjust to the unexpected and unplanned, and tolerate a degree of disorder, we were able to continue homeschooling. Within a year or so, however, his family had gone back to school. They went back because things came up that prevented them from sticking to the strict timetable they had set, and because they defined success as sticking to timetables and keeping everything in order.

So we weren't "doing school" by his definition, but by our definition we were on a roll. The children were in a weekend Chinese school. Working with a friend, we'd gotten a weekly chemistry lab course off the ground for our two families. Our children were still practicing and marching with their fife-and-drum corps. We were still doing judo. The move helped us. There was more space, so it was easier for the girls to find a quiet place to study, and for the little boys to find a place where they could make noise without fear of big sisters. We finally had enough space to shelve all our books. But when they were supposed to be helping to shelve the books, the girls kept stealing away to read them as they unearthed an old favorite or discovered a new find. We found out that the new house gave them more nooks and crannies where they could curl up with Tolstoy and Jane Austen. Meanwhile the boys, then aged two, five, and nine, were exploring the adjoining woods and backyard and making the new home their own. So we let the schedule bend as far as it had to, just as we often have when dealing with the vicissitudes of illness, new babies, visitors, travel, and floods. The schedule relaxes when it has to relax, but studies never stop, and they continue throughout the year. Once when we tried to take a summer off, the children were asking for study materials by the end of July— they said they felt dull without study. We have noticed that continuing with math through the year means that we never have to waste time reviewing. We've talked with other parents who have adopted a year-round approach for the same reason. Nonetheless, the fear that we weren't doing things "by the book" was always nagging at the back of our minds. It's hard to relax completely into the roll, but it's important to try.

- -

9/11/01

- -

We know now that we are far from the only homeschooling family that does not promptly start the new school year the Wednesday after Labor Day. I have spoken with several people who were still on vacation on September 11, 2001. That was to have been the day we commenced a new "school year," and we planned to do things the "right way": on time, on schedule, in sufficient space, with no exceptions.

I had been turning the radio off at 8:30, but had decided to leave the news on until nine as the children gathered for school. Listening to *Morning Edition* on NPR was as much a part of the morning routine as making coffee. We were there together to hear the announcer on the radio and then hear the static as the transmitter failed; to switch to the television until the signal was lost. Then we were cut off, but not from one another.

It was a least a month before we were genuinely able to focus on any regular academic work. We went to mass, checked our supplies of water and staples in case other attacks occurred, saw the smoke in the distance, observed the absence of flyovers as the air traffic was grounded, wondered if Dad would be able to get back from St. Louis, observed the dazed patience in traffic and crowds that at other times might have passed as civility. Whereas normally a driver dozing for five seconds when the light changed would be honked at, cursed, or gesticulated at rudely, for the rest of the week people waited in silence for their turns through the intersection. Not until the weekend did the honking impatience return. It was as though with a new week the issue was passed, yet we could not shake a sense of foreboding, of futility, of depression.

Much of the fall became a unit study in the Middle East and Islam. *The Great Game: The Struggle for Empire in Central Asia* and other books, and issues of *The Economist*, were devoured by the girls. All of this was in an attempt to understand the unfathomable.

Reading

Free reading was the most important factor in our daughters' education. For the boys, it was important but less dependable. It would have been much more difficult to work with the girls if they had not loved to read. Through reading, they soaked up the basics of grammar and spelling and good style, without many grammar lessons or spelling classes. We did provide a few work sheets and we did pay some attention to grammar and punctuation. But most of the children's education in these subjects came from trial and error, experience and correction. We never allow bad grammar, whether spoken or written, to pass without correction. Doing so reinforces a bad habit. If a child says something in public, when prompt correction would be embarrassing, we bring up the incident later in private. Consequently, although we very seldom "did" grammar lessons, the girls sailed through the grammar section on standardized tests by picking the answers that "sounded right."

We have been very careful to screen for both style and substance every book coming into the house. Some books are not only not worth reading, but destructive, wasting time and presenting poor models. Through careful scavenging at library and used-book sales we have rescued many older books, beautifully written, sometimes elegantly bound and illustrated, but no longer wanted. We live with thousands of adopted books.

Older books often assume a richer vocabulary and comfort with subtler and more elaborate sentence structures.

Most recently published children's literature and the current abridgments and adaptations of children's classics seem the literary equivalent of a chain restaurant's "kids' menu." Maybe there's nothing wrong with the occasional kids' menu item, but a steady diet of it is both boring and unhealthy. The same thing is true with children's literature. Some children's literature is clearly the product not of a writer but of a committee whose mandate consists of achieving both sensationalism and politically correct didacticism. There are some striking exceptions, but they are rare.

There are some useful book lists to help guide homeschool reading. We used these lists to discover books that we might have overlooked, and to help the children plan their basic reading through high school. Helpful sources include *Designing Your Own Classical Curriculum,* by Laura Berquist; *The Educated Child,* by William Bennett; *The Well-Trained Mind,* by Susan Wise Bauer and Jessie Wise; *The Language Police,* by Diane Ravitch—each of which has suggestions for all grades—and *Reading Lists for College-Bound Students,* by Doug Estell, Michele L. Satchwell, and Patricia S. Wright.

Popular Culture and Media

Reading isn't the only channel for learning, of course. Television and other media are quite useful, but we use them cautiously. Several homeschooling families in our circles have no television. We aren't such absolutists, but the default setting for our TV is "off." Television is a risky medium, capable of doing real cognitive damage (see box below). We think of it as in many ways similar to smoking. But we think that, unlike smoking, it can be beneficial in moderation. We also allow, but monitor and control access to, computer and handheld games and the Internet.

We use electronic media as a tool. When we were starting out with homeschooling in the early 1990s, we could look to public television for distance-learning shows and high-quality dramatic productions. Daytime children's programming offered an entertaining approach to literary plotlines (*Wishbone*), geography and history (*Carmen Sandiego*), science (*Bill Nye*), and math (*Square One*). We could also, in those days, look to regular network stations for reruns of ancient shows such as *I Love Lucy* and *The Honeymooners*. These were useful for simple literary analysis (plot, conflict, climax, character, parallels, subplot), good fun, and cultural allusions. Most of those old shows no longer run in our area and our television screen is dark more often than it used to be.

- -

You Don't Let Your Kids Smoke, So Why Let Them Watch TV?

- -

In 1997, flashing lights on a show broadcast in Japan sent 700 children to the hospital, many with epileptic seizures.[3] Although that case was extreme, research over the past two decades suggests that television can cause both psychological harm and physical damage to the brain. "Educational researchers say that students born into the age of television can't pay attention to lectures as well because that requires summoning up visual images themselves and they just can't do it. They've lost or never developed that ability," says Esther Thorson, professor of advertising and associate dean, graduate studies/research, at the University of Missouri School of Journalism. "I think that clearly, watching television changes the way your brain works in very important ways and I think it gets worse over time."[4]

Thorson was one of the first researchers to measure brain wave and galvanic skin responses to what she calls the "structural components of the stimulus—lightness, darkness, changes in sound from loud to soft, contrast, movement." She and her colleagues have found that such structural features can stimulate involuntary reflex responses. "For example, looming," she says. "If a ball or rock is coming toward you, you cannot not pay attention to it. You can take a looming stimulus and make it artificial on the screen of a TV set, by having a circle grow in size as if a rock were coming through the air. What we've found is that when you insert these kinds of events in ads, news, or TV programming, attention is riveted and cannot be taken away unless you pull the person away."[5]

Research presented in *Scientific American* reported that people feel "relaxed and passive" when looking at television. This was no surprise, since previous research had shown brain wave activity to be lower when viewing television than when reading.

The researchers wrote, "What is more surprising is that the sense of relaxation ends when the set is turned off, but the feelings of passivity and lowered alertness continue. Survey

(continued)

[63]

participants commonly reflect that television has somehow absorbed or sucked out their energy, leaving them depleted. They say they have more difficulty concentrating after viewing than before. In contrast, they rarely indicate such difficulty after reading." Summarizing numerous other studies, these researchers concluded that television meets the standard for substance dependence, and that television addiction is not just a metaphor.[6]

Homeschoolers watch much less television than the average American. In his 1998 study of homeschoolers, analyst Lawrence Rudner cites data indicating that almost two-thirds of homeschooled fourth-graders watch an hour or less of television per day, while only a quarter of conventionally schooled students of the same age watch so little. Almost none of the homeschooled students watch more than three hours a day, but almost 40 percent of conventionally schooled students do.[7]

In school, the pressure to watch television seems high. When our daughter was in second grade, and still attending school, she paid a social price for our television habits, because so many of the conversations depended on knowing what happened on the shows everyone else was watching. Since homeschoolers watch so little television, they tend to talk about other things—often about books, projects, or sports.

We know some homeschoolers who have gotten rid of the television altogether. Others, like us, keep the set but use it very selectively. We include cinema in our curriculum, and spend an evening or two a week watching a great movie. We also watch a few television programs that have stood the test

(continued)

of time, programs so well done or featuring such great per-
formers that it would be impoverishing to ignore them.

This puts us far out of the American mainstream with
respect to media habits. A recent study by the Kaiser Family
Foundation found that children between ages eight and eighteen average over eight hours of media exposure a day.[8] Few
seem aware of the price that children may have to pay for
their media habits. "There are many people—we see them
every day in the laboratory, we sit them down and try to get
them to read the newspaper and they can't do it," says Thorson.[9] It seems that excessive use of television and other
media has impaired their ability to make connections between words and meanings—that is, robbed them of the capacity for some kinds of thought.

Perhaps low levels of television viewing may have a lot to
do with the academic performance of homeschoolers. It's not
only that abstaining from television gives the homeschooled
students more time to study. Avoiding the cognitive damage
caused by television might even make them more able to
study. Television's cognitive risk is not yet widely accepted, of
course. But the risk of cigarettes was far from widely accepted in 1964, when the first surgeon general's report came
out. It took forty years and thousands of premature deaths
from heart disease, cancer, and emphysema before the case
was solid, unquestionable, and accepted by the public at
large. Yet people who quit smoking in 1964 probably did
themselves a favor. We think the same logic applies to television—it's habit-forming, potentially unhealthy, and not worth
the risk.

Yet video media are integral to contemporary culture. We do not isolate the children from them, but educate the children so that they can use them with mastery, not succumb to them. We weave media into our curriculum, enlivening reading, writing, arithmetic, science, and foreign language. We do use the Internet and the Web actively. The children keep in touch with many homeschooling friends by e-mail and instant messaging. We watch movies as part of our history and language studies. Cinema at its best also offers great drama, good stories, and all-round excellent entertainment. The penetration of media into our culture makes it necessary to understand the common language shaped by media. Such expressions as "Beam me up, Scotty," "If you build it they will come," and "With great power comes great responsibility" are fully intelligible only when you understand their context in *Star Trek* and *Field of Dreams* and *Spider-Man,* respectively. Understanding such allusions is necessary to follow contemporary newspapers, magazines, and other media, especially to "get" headlines and political cartoons.

As homeschoolers, we try to do more than just round up the usual suspects. We do think that a level of media literacy is necessary to be a functioning member of contemporary society. But we exercise caution in how the children achieve this degree of literacy. For example, we rarely allow young children to watch television alone. We either watch with them or delegate a considerably older sibling to do so, unless we trust the program (such trust is rare). Watching with them involves having a conversation about what is happening on the screen. We may editorialize, analyze, and vet programs in order to distance ourselves and help them develop the skills to understand both the medium and its message.

Writing Skills

We emphasize reading and seeing more than writing. We do not demand that the children write until they are mature enough to have something to say and some reason to say it in writing. Consequently, writing comes much later for them than it does for the conventionally schooled. It astonishes us to see how much writing the schools demand of young children these days. Even test-prep books for first-graders demand writing. We've done some tutoring of middle school students and we see how often these students confront more writing assignments than we think is healthy for a middle schooler. They show us notebooks with homework assignments that include responses to quotations from Herodotus, essays on "picture prompts," book reports, and more. The little middle schoolers produce what is demanded of them as well as they can, usually cranking it out in simple declarative sentences without attention to style or concrete details. One such student came to our daughter Bridget, pleading, "Help me to be more creative! My teacher says I need to be more creative."

For us, writing is not a subject assignment but an ancillary part of other activities. One of the children simply loved to write, and wrote for the sake of playing with language. The others wrote because something they wanted to do required them to write. They kept journals because they wanted to keep journals, not because we assigned it. The most important part of our writing curriculum was public speaking.

Rhetoric

Working with our homeschooled Lincoln-Douglas debate team, all three girls developed skills to write persuasive arguments supported by evidence, and to rewrite or restructure these arguments under pressure during a debate. Weekly debate practice included impromptu practice, in which they had three minutes to organize a five-point speech in response to a quotation. This practice gave them the skills and confidence they needed to compose essays under time pressure, for tests, college admissions, scholarship applications, and the like.

Our sons have begun to follow a similar path toward writing. We did not discover the opportunity of competitive rhetoric, speech, and debate until our daughters were of high school age. We incorporated rhetoric into the curriculum, and our sons began to compete in public speaking in the middle school years. Competition of a sort unavailable in most schools was a great incentive to them to memorize speeches at that age. In turn, memorization of good models of rhetoric quickly improved the way they spoke and wrote. We suspect that the pressure on students to write early may be as damaging as the pressure to read early. In any case, our patient and tactical approach seems to have served our children well.

Languages

Language study, on the other hand, begins early. Many homeschoolers emphasize Latin and Greek. We love the classics, and have worked on the basics of Latin, because it is useful to understanding English word roots. Yet our guiding principle has been to study those languages that will allow the children to communicate with a broad range of people living today. Thus, when we had the opportunity to join a Chinese school founded by immigrants from Taiwan to keep their children in touch with their native culture, we seized upon it. We had both studied Chinese while living in Asia, so we knew that we could help with the homework. We feel that it is important both to study a new language with native speakers, and to participate as fully as possible in the culture. The Chinese school was the next best thing to going to China.

We leave the choice of a second foreign language to the children. We have tried to make a wide range of opportunities available to them. Anna chose to study Spanish at the local community college. Bridget chose German; Lena, Greek; William, Italian.

When we began to homeschool the girls, the Internet was in its infancy. As time went on, though, there was an explosion of new opportunities to study languages on the Web. For example, the BBC, Deutsche Welle, and other national broadcasters offer free language courses through their websites. The BBC site is particularly impressive for the number of language courses offered. For years, because our girls expressed an interest in the language, we looked for some opportunity to study Arabic locally. Although New Jersey has a large Arab population, and mosques do offer language courses, we found that non-Muslims were not welcome in those classes. Lately, though, we have found a number of sites online where it is possible to study contemporary, conversational Arabic. In fact, there seems to be a free Web course for all but perhaps a handful of languages.

Mathematics

Ours is not a mathematical household. Because we recognize that we don't think mathematically, we have tried to come at math in a variety of ways. We do use textbooks. In fact, math is the only area in which we tolerate textbooks. We have experimented with several textbook series. We start the math curriculum with workbooks from Modern Curriculum Press. The girls used this series through the sixth grade, but the boys only through the third. We now switch from those workbooks to the Saxon Math series in the fourth grade. We work progressively but do not follow the series schedule rigidly. We begin with Math 54 in fourth grade and then skip ahead, depending on the child's needs and pace, all the way through high school. The greatest benefit of Saxon, for us, is that each lesson reviews earlier material so that no skill or knowledge gets rusty. Some homeschoolers have told us that they don't care for Saxon because they think that this review wastes time. But continuous reviewing and reinforcing of math skills is exactly what we want. We have seen too much slippage, in the past, if math is left undone for even a week, or one math skill is put aside for several lessons while another is mastered.

The single most important thing that we did for math skills was to forbid calculators until the children had thoroughly mastered all basic arithmetic, including multiplication of decimals. To speed up the calculations, they studied math shortcuts and techniques of mental math. We relied heavily on flash cards to help memorize the basic facts of addition, subtraction, multiplication, and division, and also worked with math games. We used manipulatives, in which category we include the abacus, and also constructed such projects as "Eratosthenes' Sieve," "Sisal's Challenge," and "Pascal's Triangle." We did not miss a chance to reinforce math skills in everyday life activities: cooking (the miscalculation that resulted in a flopped batch of chocolate chip cookies was a powerful incentive to greater accuracy in working with fractions), shopping (finding the best unit prices), measuring rooms for furniture or materials for sewing projects, and so on. Puzzle books and newsstand logic puzzles reinforced math skills in an amusing and social way. Having friends who liked math helped a lot, too.

Science

Science is not a class for us but a way of living. Science really starts with looking around carefully, making observations, and asking questions. We believe that one of the most important things children can learn about science is the fact that scientific knowledge is a work in progress. Doing science means seeing the facts, developing a working theory to account for them, then refining or changing or discarding that theory as more information and more precise technology becomes available. We studied the experience of Galileo in depth and detail, considering the political and spiritual ramifications of scientific inquiry, then relating what we had learned to modern controversies.

Our experience in schools tells us that the school approach to science focuses closely on textbooks and lab work. We take a different, more liberal approach. We think that it is important to look up and around more than occasionally, in order to contextualize. A major goal of our study of science is to become "scientifically literate," in order to understand and discuss any science issues of public importance. In science and in other areas, we find the Teaching Company quite a valuable resource. The *Joy of Science* lecture survey by Robert Hazen, Clarence J. Robinson Professor of Earth Sciences at George Mason University, is a fundamental part of our science curriculum. So are magazines and newspapers, not all of them strictly science magazines: *Scientific American, National Geographic, Smithsonian, The Economist,* and *Finan-*

cial Times have all contributed to our science studies. These varied sources ensure that the children learn about science in different ways and through different voices.

We attempt a similar approach with history, presenting information through reading, audiotapes, and videos and, wherever possible, through firsthand observation of historical sites and artifacts. Much of our direct experience of history and social sciences has come through travel. From the beginning we knew that one of the best reasons to homeschool was that it gave us the chance to hit the road.

Serendipity and Randomness in Homeschooling

As we mentioned earlier, we began homeschooling by using a curriculum company and umbrella school, but this soon became less an aid than an impediment to our efforts. During the first year, Martine filed her quarterly lesson plans and sent in her work samples and got feedback, sometimes puzzling. For example, the mentor strongly recommended phonics for a third-grader whose verbal achievement was already test-scored at the high school level. A new pregnancy, and then a new baby, interfered with scheduled lesson plans. After a while, instead of planning the work ahead of time and submitting the schedules to the mentor, she found herself forensically reconstructing what she had covered in the course of the quarter, and submitting the reconstruction.

Over the years, we have learned that many homeschooling families follow a pattern similar to our own. They begin with a structured curriculum and follow it for a year or two. Those families that plan to reenter the school system at some point are likely to adhere closely to such curricula, because they make the transition back to school easier. Yet there is a real downside to the structured curricula. The more that home-schoolers mimic school, the less they stand to benefit from the freedom and spontaneity, the serendipity and random-ness, the surprise and discovery that homeschooling can offer.

Families that persevere in homeschooling may rely on structured curricula only long enough to gain the confidence they need to take a more creative approach. One friend of ours refers to "car schooling," describing the situations in which the children do a good chunk of their studying, and the mother a good deal of instruction, en route from one ac-tivity to another. Many homeschoolers find that the automo-bile is a great venue for education. Books on tape, lectures on CD, educational programs on DVD can all help make time in a traffic jam productive, even stimulating. In our case, time in the car provides a captive audience and a time when the family "wanderers" have no choice but to stay put.

What with library expeditions, museums, trips, and other activities, the homeschool curriculum began to move like the wind, shifting in unanticipated directions. For example, as we finished our second year of homeschooling, the new di-rectors of the Plainfield library decided to cleanse the shelves of many of the older books in order to make way for new col-lections. Classics were going for pennies. We accumulated a home library of history, literature, and art books, not to mention a comprehensive classical music collection on vinyl records, obsolete in the view of the directors but wonderful to us. Not long after, a nearby pricey prep school also opted to dispose of older titles. Our library expanded further. We discovered that book sales were a frequent and regular occurrence in our area, and we became frequent and regular visitors to these. With all those books and all that music around the house, the children could always find something to interest them. The reasonable thing to do was to let them follow their interests where their interests led. Was it homeschooling when less and less of it was taking place at home, and what was taking place at home had little in common with conventional schooling?

Physical education had scarcely been part of the curriculum at the school the children had attended, but we believed it was indispensable. We joined the YMCA and enrolled the girls in swimming. Some time later, we discovered the Cranford Judo & Karate Club, and the opportunity to train with Yoshisada Yonezuka, one of the world's judo greats. Judo provided an opportunity for the children not only to enjoy a regular physical activity but also to educate their bodies, and through the fact of competition, their minds and hearts. Our daughter Anna eventually wrote her college admission essay on what she had learned when, having broken her collarbone doing randori, she fought her own fear to come back and compete again.

Background and Foreground: Music

Athletics, music, literature, science, and mathematics have not been distinct and compartmentalized subjects in our home-schooling curriculum. They were essential parts of a whole, often interpenetrating and informing one another. Our appetite for music was omnivorous: classical, jazz, Elvis, the Beatles, Dylan, even some rap, even Japanese pop and Chinese opera and more. There is no music to which we wouldn't listen and from which we couldn't learn something. A trip through the Midwest took us to Cleveland's Rock and Roll Hall of Fame and Memphis's Sun Studio, Rock N Soul Museum, and National Civil Rights Museum. Our understanding of the history of the civil rights struggle would have been incomplete without the context that the history of popular music provided.

After overcoming our initial shock at recognizing that the arrival of the Beatles in the United States was now *history,* we realized that any study of history has to include popular mu-

- -

God Bless America

- -

Just after the 2000 election, we went to see George W. Bush stop in Plainfield, New Jersey. The visit was surprising, and not very widely publicized. There were no schoolchildren assembled to see the president. The only children in the crowd were ours and those of another homeschooling family.

> The destination was an urban church that our girls knew
> because they had volunteered there and had also taken
> classes there. Outside the church was a disgruntled crowd.
> The Supreme Court hadn't really decided the election until
> December; George W. Bush had just been inaugurated a few
> weeks previously. Plainfield was a solidly Democratic city and
> feelings were strong. We had come so that the children could
> see something of politics in action. The girls had brought
> their fifes with them, and as the Bush haters and the handful
> of Bush supporters jeered at each other, they started to play
> "God Bless America." The jeering stopped. Both sides started
> singing together. It was both touching and instructive.

sic. Songs often reflect the spirit of a time, and convey more
of the color of historical events than any written record can.
On a visit to a historical site, we bought some tapes of folk
songs from the Revolutionary War, the French and Indian
War, the Westward Expansion, and the Gold Rush, and the
children learned history by hearing, then by singing those
songs. Eventually, the children joined a local fife-and-drum
corps, learned the instruments, and began to march in parades. Music was, we thought, integral to a good education,
but they learned much more than music from the corps. They
learn something fundamental about how America came to be
and how it works.

Fife-and-drum became an extremely important part of
our social studies and music curriculum. Fife-and-drum
corps have a devoted following in the New England and Mid-

Atlantic states, and many corps, like ours, rely on income from parades to cover expenses. Our corps participated in a dozen parades a year, regardless of heat, wind, rain, or snow. Only lightning stops the parades. So the children learned how to soldier on in difficult circumstances. They know the importance of working as a group, the discipline of marching the distance, the encouragement of the drumbeat and the fife.

But marching in parades also opens a window on politics and sociology. The children have seen the differences in the crowds from one community to another. They have seen politicians up close, and learned to take their measure. At one parade, our eight-year-old observed that a gubernatorial candidate was only marching and shaking hands on the shady side of the street. In the candidate's favor, it was a very hot day. The children, who were marching in the sun, knew that. Another politician nearly knocked one daughter down the stairs as he pushed to get through a door ahead of her. He

The Community College Advantage

Community college classes provided an opportunity to demonstrate quantifiable success in various subjects well before the children were technically college age. This kind of success has been important because we have always expected that the children would go on to further college and perhaps graduate studies. We don't require or demand this of them, but we do want them to be able to make that choice if it suits them.

Community colleges can provide great bargains. Our local community college, Raritan Valley, offered a concurrent program for high school students charging only $100 for the first course per term. We knew that the girls' concurrent credits would improve their academic profiles for the most selective schools, even though these schools might not recognize all the credits. At most state schools the "early credits" would translate into advanced standing. Our ultimate fallback plan for college has been for our children to top off their concurrent credits at the community college, maintaining a high GPA, then transfer to finish the undergraduate degree. Many colleges offer a grant for transfer students who are members of Phi Theta Kappa, the honor society for community college students.

Through the end of high school Magdalen took an array of introductory art classes at the community college, but by midway through her last year she had determined that she was not interested in pursuing this as a major field. Having the opportunity to investigate this through the community college early on probably saved us thousands of dollars and several years' time; she did not have to switch majors or institutions as so many students do nowadays.

was so selfish in that unguarded moment that it seemed much in character when he very publicly betrayed his wife, family, electorate, and office a while later.

Ever since the children were babies, they have gone to political events. Each of them came with us into the voting booth at some point so they could see how voting works and understand the process. They also go to rallies and debates and town meetings, where they are usually the only children present. We encourage them to ask reasonable and relevant questions, and a candidate's reasonable reaction to their questions is not irrelevant to how we vote. Some of the candidates will take time to discuss an issue even with a child. Others are busy with more important thoughts. We consider that to be a character issue in a candidate. The children also learned about character issues in the electorate when, as teenagers, they volunteered to distribute literature for campaigning candidates. Standing outside grocery stores or shopping malls, they've been cussed at and insulted by middle-aged people who didn't like the candidate they represented. They were surprised by the lack of civility—but educated by it. They were also surprised by the number of people who said they were just going to vote party line because they always had. This has given them a realistic sense of the electorate, and it has helped to inform the classes they've taken in college.

High School as Homeschool

As our daughters approached their high school years, we faced the tension between our commitment to freedom and the fact that at the end of high school there would be a college application process requiring documentation and attestation of achievements. Ultimately, debate and the community college helped our daughters to recognize that they could achieve as much as or more than conventional high school students. In fact, they had learned all they really needed to know by the time they entered their teens. For them, high school became a process of recognizing what they knew, expressing it, and gathering the necessary proof to submit to college admissions officers.

That's not to say they stopped learning, of course. They continued to study philosophy as an accompaniment to their involvement in Lincoln-Douglas debate. They continued to work on Chinese, and to develop their study of music. They continued to work through the Saxon math series. They had achieved basic scientific literacy through our homeschooling curriculum. However, they would need lab courses in order to apply to selective colleges. Our community college provided those. Community college professors were also very helpful about writing recommendation letters that gave a great deal of comfort to college-admissions officers.

Because we knew they would have to document their achievement for the college-application process, they began to take standardized tests in what we considered to be their sophomore year. Thanks to their wide reading, they were able to score high on the various language arts and social studies SAT Subject Tests and Advanced Placement tests. Like other high school students, they took the Preliminary Scholastic Aptitude Test in their junior year and, of course, the SAT or ACT. Two of them were National Merit Commended Scholars and the third was a National Merit Finalist.

CHAPTER THREE TAKEAWAYS

✓ We let the schedule bend as far as it has to.

✓ We study math throughout the year, so we don't waste time reviewing after a summer break.

✓ Reading lets our daughters learn grammar, spelling, and style, without many grammar lessons or spelling classes.

✓ We have been careful to screen for both style and substance every book coming into the house.

✓ We use electronic media and educate the children to master them, but not succumb to them.

✓ The most important part of our writing curriculum was public speaking.

✓ The children must know their arithmetic before they may use calculators.

✓ Science is not a class for us, but a way of living, looking around, making observations, and asking questions.

✓ Music was indispensable to our study of history.

✓ Community colleges are great resources for homeschoolers.

FOUR

A Focus on the Person

Our youngest child, Blaise, started reading at age eight. I could say "didn't start reading until age eight," because, by school standards, that's pretty late. Children who wait that long to read fall behind in school. Many parents seem to pride themselves on early-reading children. We even know homeschoolers who brag about the child who begins reading at age three or four. When you Google the phrase "early readers," you find scores of links to websites full of information about how to teach children to read early.

But we're delighted by the fact that Blaise took his time about getting around to reading. The fact that he couldn't read didn't hurt his education at all. In fact, it helped him immensely. Long before he could read, he knew the names of a couple of dozen dinosaur species, their dietary habits, which ones flourished in the Triassic, the Jurassic, and the Cretaceous, the broad outlines of the extinction story, where on earth the best fossils of each had turned up, and how paleontologists went about finding them. Although our backyard hadn't produced any famous fossils, Blaise allowed that might just be because no one had dug there, so he spent days in our backyard and on the woody hillside behind the house, digging up rocks that he said might be teeth or bones or anything— you never know until you check it out. He scrubbed with toothbrushes, tapped with hammers, and accumulated a small collection of items for further investigation. He learned most of his paleontologist's craft from tapes and DVDs, although some came from books his mother and sisters or brothers read to him and from trips to museums.

Originally we had expected that Blaise would begin reading earlier than any of his siblings. He had played with word and picture puzzles and Boggle Jr. from the age of two, and used phonics software later. He enjoyed lining up the letters to match the puzzle pictures and would amuse himself with this all morning while his older siblings worked nearby.

He was the earliest, at age three, to come to Martine saying, "Mommy, I can spell a word." While Martine poured coffee, he pulled letter magnets out of the basket hanging on the refrigerator, two *w*'s, and one *m,* which he flipped to show *www.* (Blaise is the only family member born after the Web was a fact of life.) As he entered his fourth year, Blaise was also doing a great job of interpreting icons on road signs, and spotting commercial logos over our shoulders in the newspapers. With such initiative on his part and reinforcement on her part, Martine was sure he would be a precocious reader.

Reinforcement was a rule of the house—a toddler who wanted reading time got it, even if it meant interrupting other work or plans. We also read Dickens at the dinner table, initially because a dieting parent finished eating quickly, didn't want to leave the family table, and found reading a good way to take the mind off food. Setting reading in a social context is critical, according to researcher David Elkind, who notes the importance of personal contact and attention. "What is crucial to beginning to read is the child's attachment to an adult who spends time reading to or with the child. The motivation for reading, which is a difficult task, is social."[1]

"Late" Reading

We had a family tradition of reading parties to mark the transition to literacy. The first time each child read a first book on his or her own, we celebrated with a reading party that could last all night. We thought Blaise was within a month of reading his first book when he was four and began to make a list of the snacks for his reading party. But he hung back, much to our consternation. We tried to help him make the jump by using phonics or other language-development work sheets, but he didn't jump. Couldn't he? Wouldn't he? After many anxious months, information that Martine received at a homeschooling conference emboldened her to delay reading instruction.

You have to search a bit for the research suggesting that teaching children to read early may be bad for them and that children who read late may have an advantage. But there is

Risks of Early Reading

*David Elkind, professor of child study and
senior resident scholar at the Lincoln Filene
Center, Tufts University, cites numerous
studies showing that "adolescents who
were introduced to reading late were more
enthusiastic, spontaneous readers than
were those who were introduced to reading
early," and "children confronted with the
task of learning to read before they have
the requisite mental abilities can develop
long-term learning difficulties."[2]*

such research. We were relieved to discover it, because it confirmed what we had already begun to sense from our own experience with six children.

Because we homeschool, the fact that Blaise himself couldn't read a page in a book until he was almost eight years old was no obstacle to learning. On the contrary, his education included other experiences so rich that it's fair to say learning to read might have interfered with his education.

Blaise could see deer moving through the woods behind our house, or a bluebird perched in a tree, long before the rest of us could. His eye scanned the woods and noted differences in patterns or movement. He could scan a stretch of ground and see an interesting rock all but buried in the clay. When he finally did begin to read he scanned the pages the same way. The Evelyn Woods speed-reading course, popular when I was in high school, began by insisting that in order to read faster, you had to unlearn the word-by-word reading technique most children learned in school, and then learn to scan the pages. Blaise never had to unlearn how to read slowly in order to learn how to read fast. Two months after he started reading, he read the entire *Chronicles of Narnia*, explaining, "I don't want to see the *Lion, the Witch and the Wardrobe* movie until I have read the books."

We wonder whether he would now read so well if he had spent so many hours, instead of fossil hunting and deer spotting, scrunched in a chair sounding out the letters in a book. He is a remarkably fast and voracious reader, enjoys reading, and spends hours at it. In fact, now that he spends so much time reading, we worry that he no longer goes out and looks around as much as he used to. We recognize what we didn't know before—that there is a price you pay for reading, that reading demands a trade-off. Early reading takes a toll. It opens some doors but may close others. So early reading is not all good news.

When we began to homeschool, we did not understand such trade-offs. Of course, one of the advantages of a large family is that the more children you have around you, the more you learn about children. (And about yourself for that matter.) When our first son, Billy, was four years old and showed no interest in learning to read, we worried that he would fall behind. Martine was anxious, because Billy would be the first child never to have set foot in a school. His sisters had picked up reading with the help of the parish school. But Billy would be entirely her responsibility. In order to "teach" him to read, she had saved his sisters' work sheets from preschool and kindergarten and supplemented them with phonics workbooks.

But Billy wasn't interested in reading at all. As Tammany boss George Washington Plunkitt had done, Billy "seen his opportunities and he took 'em." He loved to play ball, any kind of ball, with anything that even looked like a ball. He always had. When he was a toddler, if his mother came home from the grocery with a cabbage in the bag, he'd find it and roll it around the floor. Martine, homeschooling his older sisters and taking care of his younger brother, might only notice that Billy had slipped away from his work when she heard the basketball bouncing outside, and the sound of boys' voices.

Clearly he loved action, so Martine found Dr. Seuss workbooks that invited the child to use stickers, to underline, to X out and otherwise manipulate text. Controlling text was much more appealing than merely copying it, so Billy began reading "on schedule."

Boys and Girls

Boys are different. Throughout the seventies and eighties, I had been instructed that this was not so, and was rudely surprised. I found that while one and even two boys could be "managed," the arrival of the third precipitated a tipping point which masculinized our household, even though by the numbers we were evenly divided, male and female.

Our homeschooling experience with boys has been considerably different from that with the girls, and the difference is greater than learning styles or birth order would dictate. The most important differences are these: The boys are less likely to pursue an objective if they don't see the point. They are goal-oriented. They want to know that you are watching.

This need for a maternal audience seems to be hardwired. Finally, while the girls (our girls, anyway) would curl up with a book by default, the boys would chase one another, or play cars or ball. There is nothing wrong with this, but the difference provided the girls with an enormous verbal advantage while we had to consciously work with the boys to reach the same level.

Martine

Why should it have worried us that a four-year-old did not want to sit at a desk and do the kind of work given to school-children his age? It is an absurd concern.

Inability to read need be no handicap when homeschooling. Of course, children in the school system have to read early. But that's just because the demands of the school system, the production process of the institution, make reading necessary. Most schools rely so heavily on written textbooks and written homework assignments that if schoolchildren cannot read, they cannot learn.

Multiple Intelligences:
Demands of Learning Versus Demands of School

There is a big and very important difference between things children need to do in order to learn and things children need to do in order to perform in school. Different children learn at different speeds and in different ways. There are many ways to learn, but schools ignore most of them. So schools may be very good for a few children who happen to learn in the ways that schools emphasize, but very bad for many other children.

The term "multiple intelligences" was coined by Howard Gardner, the John H. and Elisabeth A. Hobbs Professor of Cognition and Education at the Harvard Graduate School of Education. The recipient of a MacArthur Fellowship and of numerous honorary degrees, Gardner proposed a new approach to education, called "individual-centered schooling," that would tailor each child's education to his or her unique intelligence. He wrote, "Uniform education mandates the same curricula for all children, taught in the same way, and with the same tests administered regularly to all children—while the students need not wear uniforms, they are otherwise treated as interchangeable with one another. Whatever its utility at other times or other eras, I believe that uniform schooling has little to recommend it in the America of today, while individual centered education fits well our pluralistic and rapidly changing society."[3]

Gardner argues that intelligence is merely the ability to understand and use information in some way that a culture or society values, and that there are as many kinds of intelligence as there are valuable ways to understand and use information. IQ tests and their offspring (such as the SAT) measure one or two kinds of intelligence. But Gardner suggests that there are several other forms of intelligence that such tests do not measure, among them:

- Musical intelligence: solves problems of harmony, rhythm, and musical structure.

- Spatial intelligence: solves problems involving space and motion through space. Useful to fighter pilots, graphic designers, architects, and corporate reorganizers who draw and redraw organization charts.

- Physical intelligence: processes information and gets results using the body. Indispensable to surgeons, athletes, and handicraft artisans.

- Naturalist intelligence: the ability to make sense of similarities and differences among clouds, plants, animals, rocks, and so forth. A life-or-death matter to our hunting and farming ancestors, naturalist intelligence may have a role in contemporary society when it is necessary to distinguish among consumer goods.

- People intelligence: the ability to make sense of oneself and of others, to understand relationships, to know what people are likely to do, to work with others.

- Existential intelligence: addresses the ultimate questions of meaning, spirituality, philosophy, and so on.[4]

Individual-centered education means meeting the child where the child is, developing the kinds of intelligence a child has, instead of demanding that the child sink or swim on the basis of just one kind of intelligence. Reading Howard

Gardner after we'd been homeschooling for years was quite a revelation. This is more or less the kind of educational approach that we have taken in our homeschooling curriculum. It is always comforting to have what one is doing confirmed by experts as what one ought to be doing. It's just too bad that we didn't recognize this when we started to homeschool, because that recognition might have spared us some anxiety. We worried about all sorts of things, and that kind of worrying looks ridiculous in retrospect.

Because homeschooling can adapt its pedagogy and curriculum to each child, proceeding at the pace and in the manner best suited to his or her personality, the homeschooled child who is easily distracted, very active, or just not interested in reading can still make fast educational progress. Among our acquaintances is a woman who homeschooled her daughter through the elementary years. The girl did not really begin to read until she was almost twelve years old. (She was struggling through early readers while she shopped with our daughters at a library sale.) Late reading didn't prevent her from achieving National Merit Commended Scholar status six years later.

When you homeschool, you don't have to read in order to learn. Our children learned from films, audiotapes, CDs, DVDs; from bird-watching, fishing, bug collecting, berry picking, fungus foraging; from music, talking, digging up rocks, taking apart old radios; from camping out, visiting Civil War battlefields, playing basketball, doing judo; from shopping for cars and for a house, planning to move, and gardening; from cooking, eating, and conversation at mealtimes.

Context of the Person

Our educational goal is to equip our children for the free pursuit of truth through virtue. This is a goal that schools do not and cannot share. Their rules and operating constraints do not permit pursuit of virtue in the core curriculum, because virtue requires judgments of right and wrong that would surely be controversial. Any code of virtues must have roots in some sense of the meaning of life and the nature of humanity, and that means making some judgments about ultimate things—again, too controversial for schools. Moreover, as virtue is something that one can only learn from good models and from constant practice, schools in order to teach it would have to be full of people at least trying to pursue it (honestly trying means acknowledging failure and trying again, again, again).

Yet without what schools by their rules and operating structures cannot allow, education becomes something degenerate and denatured. Education, real education, must take place in the context of a personal relationship. This relationship between persons becomes the foundation for another kind of relationship, the relationship of the student with the process of learning, with a tradition of learning, and with other persons who reach and may be reached through that process and tradition. These relationships shape the student. They help the student develop, through emulation, the personal characteristics of attention and imagination and diligence and dedication that are necessary to *discern,* to relate to, and, eventually, to teach others the way of learning.

In his essay "Tradition and the Individual Talent," T. S. Eliot wrote, "What happens is a continual surrender of himself as he is at the moment to something which is more valuable. The progress of an artist is a continual self-sacrifice." That is equally true of the student, and only through personal relationship can the student learn how to see both what is more valuable than himself and how to go about making that self-sacrifice. This is why small classes are so important—they allow for personal relationships that are impossible in a crowd. Education should develop the person. It should develop the person so the person can in turn make a gift of personhood, a gift of self, what Eliot called a "continual self-sacrifice." When we have studied a musical instrument, or tai chi, or judo, even cooking, real instruction has come through emulation, through seeing one who is more proficient do it and then trying to imitate the action. Similarly, there are so many little details involved in developing as a learning person that it is almost impossible to capture them in any other way than emulation. Schools seldom teach this way.

When Anna and Magdalen briefly attended the local high school, one of their classes was AP English literature. If it is fair to infer the purpose of a class from how it is taught, the purpose of this class was not to form a relationship with the teacher and, through her, a relationship with literature. The purpose clearly seemed the extraction and memorization of certain facts in preparation for a test. I should say, if it is not already clear from the preceding chapters, that we are a reading family, and the girls had already learned to relate to literature. They had learned that relationship through their relationship with their parents and their sisters and brothers. They not only read but they talked about what they discovered in reading, and in talking they learned about what they might discover if they looked at what they had read in a slightly different way. We all learned through such conversations.

Never having attended schools beyond kindergarten, Anna and Magdalen were expecting to find something similar in the literature class in high school. So they were genuinely shocked to find out that many of their fellow students did not even bother to read the novels assigned for this class, but just read SparkNotes or CliffsNotes to get the facts they'd need for the test.

In order to make the point that it was the facts that mattered, and just these facts, the teacher wrote them on the board, and emphasized that everyone should copy them because they would be on the test. When the class read *The Great Gatsby*, for example, the teacher wrote every color on the board and next to the color wrote what every color "symbolized." Lena told us afterward (very reasonably, we thought), "Sometimes a color in a novel doesn't symbolize anything. Sometimes it's just a color, just there to make a scene, but the teacher didn't seem to understand this, and didn't want to discuss it."

The students in this class were learning a kind of perversion of relationship, a relationship not to literature but to the institution of school. They reminded me a little of the baby monkeys whose mothers were replaced by wire or cloth dolls in the famous series of experiments by psychological researcher Harry F. Harlow.[5] They were learning an absence of relationship to literature through an absence of relationship to a teacher, who never really had time to discuss literature or alternative interpretations and responses to literary work.

I thought my daughters might just have had bad luck of the draw and gotten an exceptionally unimaginative literature teacher. But I learned otherwise from some of my students in a weekend writing class I instructed at our local Chinese school. These students were among the best-performing students at some of the best public schools in New Jersey. When I presented them with classic essays, they seemed lost, unable to relate personally to, or discuss, what they read. When I asked them how much reading they did, they told me that they seldom read anything that was not required for school. Their reason for reading was not to form a personal relationship with a literary tradition but rather to get what was required for tests. Their relationship was entirely with the requirements of an institution, utterly depersonalized, and therefore in fact no relationship at all.

How Schools Harm Education

When the development of the person ceases to be the purpose and the way of education, as it has in our schools, then the process of education is no longer education at all. The word "education" is related to the Latin *ex ducere,* meaning "to lead out." But schooling as we know it is not a "leading out" at all. It is a "leading in," a kind of servitude or confinement in which the student becomes the object by which an institution furthers its own agenda.

From time to time evidence of this breaks into the headlines. For example, students sitting for the New York Regents' English Language Arts exam in 2002 found an exam that included sections of literature stripped of meaning and emotional resonance. The Regents had censored references to Judaism from a story by Isaac Bashevis Singer, including the line "Jews are Jews and Gentiles are Gentiles," even though that was Singer's point. A piece from Annie Dillard's *An American Childhood,* as originally written, showed how she had learned about race in America through her visits to a library "in the Negro section of town." The Regents cut the racial references, which is to say, cut out the meaning of the piece. A similar process occurs with textbooks, as publishers aim to meet standards set by many different and often mutually contradictory agendas nationwide.[6]

The lesson that many children leave schools with is to manipulate rules with more or less cleverness for more or less short-term gains, how to focus on test scores and GPAs instead of on truth, how to exercise low cunning instead of high learning. This is not a reflection on the children, but rather the outcome to be expected when the school neglects the social aspect of learning by shortchanging a real development of relationships that could foster a more humane approach to life. As Stephen Covey writes, "In the short run, in an artificial social system such as school, you may be able to get by if you learn how to manipulate the man-made rules, to 'play the

game. . . .' Eventually, if there isn't deep integrity and fundamental character strength, the challenges of life will cause
true motives to surface and human relationship failure will
replace short-term success."[7]

The development of the person through virtue, leading to
a gift of oneself in service to others, seems to us the whole
purpose of human life. In ghettos and barrios, where the de-
personalizing brutality of our economic system is most evident,
school dropout rates are highest. It seems not unreasonable
at all for children to drop out of a school system that secures
them neither jobs nor freedom.[8]

Dropout rates were not the only indication that the
schools were failing our African-American neighbors in Plainfield. Our sons played with children in the neighborhood, and
were surprised by their antipathy toward reading and study.
More than race, this drew a line between them. There were a
few African-Americans among the growing number of homeschoolers in the area, and with them there was no such line.

We wondered how this option might better serve our
neighbors and eventually learned of Joyce Burges, founder of
National Black Home Educators. Like us, she had first attempted to work with the system, but found that the school
system's priorities were not hers, that its definition of an appropriate education for her children would constrain rather
than develop their potential. The experience of Burges and
other pioneering black homeschoolers shows how African-
Americans can unshackle themselves from a system that
badly disserves their children.

Joyce Burges, Founder, National Black Home Educators

Joyce Burges and her husband, Eric, founded National Black Home Educators (NBHE) in 2000 to bring the option of homeschooling to the attention of African-Americans. "They're seeing so much misery in public schools," she says. With three children in public school, she had been president of one school's parent-teacher organization and chairman of the advisory board at another. "They say, 'Why don't you just stay in the system and help it?' But that's the biggest myth, the biggest lie. They don't want your help. They don't want you there—or if they do want you there, they don't want you there in the capacity of an equal. They want you there to make copies of one math book for thirty children, to raise money for much-needed equipment, to babysit their classrooms. They want you there just to be a mindless person. But they don't want you there to give advice on how to teach—and a lot of them need it!"

Homeschooling may be the best chance African-Americans have to free their children from the dangers of the school system, especially the urban school system. Negative socialization is one such danger. Another is labeling and stereotyping. Says Burges, "I think homeschooling is becoming more positive for African-American families because we're seeing boys labeled by the system. They're ADD or ADHD or BD or labeled really badly, and that record follows them until they decide to drop out, which is in the early high school years."

(continued)

Homeschooling addresses those problems by bringing the family closer together. "It forces parents to become interactive with their children, to pay attention to their children, the strengths as well as the weaknesses. It forces parents to be parents again."

But relatively few African-American families and educators recognize those advantages, in part because of the perception that homeschooling is something that only whites can do, and that whites often do it precisely in order to escape integrated schools. When Burges herself started to homeschool, it seemed at first to be a lonely choice. "There were no other blacks homeschooling that I knew of. I went into the white society to get information. There were two or three families reaching out for something different, as I was. They embraced us and invited us to their homes, and we invited them to ours." Eventually her husband became the president of the predominantly white homeschooling association in Louisiana.

The discovery that blacks can and do homeschool successfully doesn't silence critics of homeschooling within the black community, but Burges is used to dealing with them. "They just go to the next tier, which is 'You're not qualified.' That's another myth. I am the mother. I'm responsible. These are our children. We have a parental right to homeschool." The only qualification the parents really need, Burges affirms, is love for their children and a willingness to teach what they know.

Critics charge that American high schools fail in the mission of educating children. There's plenty of evidence to support them. For example, tests of science achievement administered in 2006 found that only 54 percent of high school seniors met basic standards and only 18 percent were proficient, and instead of improving, students had gotten worse. Ten years earlier, 57 percent had met basic standards.[9] American students' math skills lagged those of students in many other countries.[10] It's commonplace to see such reports in the press, usually followed by calls to do something about the schools. But betting on schools to succeed at the mission of education is like betting on a school bus to win the Daytona 500. That hasn't been their mission. They weren't designed to do that job. Schools aren't and have never been mainly focused on academic excellence—people who advocated academic excellence were only one interest group, and for most of the twentieth century they were all but irrelevant.

Indeed, although it may sound strange to people unfamiliar with the history of American education, public high schools have never aimed to educate each child. Several researchers who examined the development of schools in the twentieth century have concluded that the main objective of schools was just to please and entertain. Schools and educational reformers followed the money, just as consumer-goods marketers do, and kept trying to adapt their curriculum to make it more appealing to their customers—students and parents.[11] Academic subjects were unpopular among educators because they seemed unpopular among students, so many educators actually tried to downplay or get rid of academics.

One of the most powerful educational reform efforts of the mid-twentieth century, life-adjustment education, aimed at removing traditional academics from schools altogether, at least for the majority of students.[12] As one proponent of life-adjustment education wrote in the *Bulletin of the National Association of Secondary School Principals,* "We shall some-day accept the thought that it is just as illogical to assume that every boy must be able to read as it is that each one must be able to perform on a violin, that it is no more reasonable to require that each girl shall spell well than it is that each one shall bake a good cherry pie. When adults finally realize that fact, everyone will be happier . . . and schools will be nicer places in which to live."[13]

How many people stop to think about what the school is doing, or why? Who considers the purpose of the school cur-riculum? What is it? Is the school's purpose your purpose too? How does the school measure success? Is that how you measure success? Few people seem to ask such questions.

The difference between homeschooling and public school-ing is mainly a matter of focus. There are many different ap-proaches to homeschooling, many different curricula and teaching styles. But they all have in common the practice of education through personal relationship. How can a home-schooling mother with very little formal education and very little money educate a child to a higher standard than public schools with budgets measured in the millions? Primarily by providing a dimension of personal relationship that fosters genuine learning. Homeschooling always occurs in the con-text of a personal relationship, sometimes of many personal relationships. Homeschooling multiplies personal relation-ships through homeschooling groups and networks. As these personal relationships form and develop, homeschooling appears more and more unlike the stereotype of isolationist individuals cutting themselves off from the mainstream. On the contrary, homeschooling is an intensely personal and social system, one that is powerfully human in its creativity, its intelligence, its responsiveness to change.

On a summery September day my wife, Martine, was waiting outside the library to take our daughter Lena home from her part-time job. As Martine passed the time by watching the passersby, a parsnip swallowtail butterfly beat its dark wings to the red petunias planted in a circular bed near the library entrance, floating, landing, seeming to quiver with delight as it found a new flower, then dancing up on a gust of wind only to whirl back to the late flowers. Martine has always loved swallowtail butterflies and often, when she sees one, gives a little cry and grabs my arm and points it out.

Under any circumstances a swallowtail would have been remarkable to her, but this swallowtail at the close of summer, turning and fluttering around and above the red annuals, poignant fading sunlight sparkling from blue-rimmed wings, seemed to cry to her. Lena's sisters had gone off to college, and she was about to begin the college-application process herself. Martine had homeschooled her daughters from primary school through high school, and now, as she looked back, her time with the girls seemed to have passed as swiftly as the season of a swallowtail.

She noticed that she seemed to be the only person paying attention to the colors twirling there among the flowers. People came and went along the walk by the flower bed but they hurried, preoccupied. They fumbled with keys or books or cellphones, their eyes fixed in a tense blank absence that goes with thinking of what happened this morning or what has to happen this afternoon, or with thinking, "What I should have said was . . ." or "If he does that one more time . . ." Distracted by urgent fantasies of a past no longer present and a future they might never see, they bustled along, blind to the momentous whirl of red and blue and sunlight in the flower bed at their feet. None of them even seemed to notice the dancing swallowtail. After a few minutes, Martine began to make little wagers with herself, thinking, "Surely this person will see what I see."

There was one tantalizing moment of suspense: A young Asian girl came out of the library with her arms full of books. They looked like required reading for the school year that had just begun. She paused for a moment at the flower bed almost as if she sensed something. She even glanced apprehensively from one side to the other. She gave every hint that she was about to see—but they were false hints, because the girl's eye did not catch, and she looked away, and walked off. Maybe she had just been wondering whether she had forgotten something and then suddenly remembered that she had not; whatever she was thinking, her mind was somewhere else.

And then Lena came through the door, hurrying because she was late getting out, and scanned the parking lot for the family car. Suddenly she saw the urgent wings beating color from the air above the flowers, and her eyes lit up and her face beamed with bittersweet joy at the transient moment.

Education has helped the children make a better living. By a better living we mean not more money but a life with more life in it.

Our homeschooling "curriculum" included mushroom hunting in spring and fall. Home from college for Christmas break, Lena's sisters were talking about fungi they had noticed in and around the trees on their campuses. Anna said she'd puzzled about the identity of a big mushroom growing in a stump alongside the walkway to her dorm at Brown. "It looked a little like hen-of-the-woods, but a little like artist's conk," she told us. "We were talking in my dorm and I mentioned it, and the people I was talking with looked at me and said, 'What mushroom?' They said they'd never noticed anything. I was surprised. It was right alongside the walk! How could anyone miss it?"

CHAPTER FOUR TAKEAWAYS

✓ Late reading need not be an obstacle to learning, if learning is not classroom-based but rather includes an array of rich experiences.

✓ Early reading can take a toll. It opens some doors, but may close others, by centering learning on a page.

✓ One of the advantages of a large family is that the more children you have around you of various ages, the more you can learn about children. (And about yourself, for that matter.)

✓ Children in the school system have to read early because most schools rely so heavily on written textbooks and written homework assignments that if schoolchildren cannot read, they cannot learn.

✓ The things that children need to do in order to learn and the things that children need to do in order to perform in school are quite different.

✓ Homeschooling can adapt its pedagogy and curriculum to each child, proceeding at the pace and in the manner best suited to his or her personality.

✓ Authentic education takes place in the immediate context of a personal relationship, and extends to a tradition of learning.

✓ Education should develop the person. It should develop the person so the person can in turn make a gift of personhood, a gift of self, what T. S. Eliot called a "continual self-sacrifice."

✓ When the development of the person ceases to be the purpose and the way of education, as it has in our schools, then the process of education is no longer education at all.

✓ The development of the person through virtue, leading to a gift of oneself in service to others, seems to us the whole purpose of human life, and therefore the purpose of education.

✓ Homeschooling may be the best chance that African-Americans have to free their children from the dangers of the school system, especially the urban school system.

✓ Although it may sound strange to people unfamiliar with the history of American education, public high schools have never aimed to educate each child.

✓ Parents may want to stop to ponder what the school is doing, and why? Who considers the purpose of the school curriculum? What is it? Is the school's purpose your purpose too? How does the school measure success? Is that how you measure success?

FIVE

Watching the Volcano: Vision, Mission, Values

One day a newspaper carried the story about Pak Darto, who sits in a village in Indonesia and sleeplessly watches Mount Merapi, Indonesia's most active volcano. About a decade ago, a fast-moving cloud of hot gas swept down from the Mountain of Fire—the English meaning of Merapi—incinerating dozens of his neighbors. The people in his village do not trust the government's system to alert them in time to flee an eruption, because the sound of the government's siren takes too long to reach them. Yet although Mount Merapi has been leaking gas and lava, they have refused to evacuate and abandon their homes to looters, because the volcano may not erupt now after all. Having lived by the Mountain of Fire for generations, they feel confident that they know it better than anyone else—and they especially respect Darto, who watches constantly, and who has a special connection with the mysteries of nature and spirits. The villagers trust him to warn them when it is time to move. Darto is teaching his son to watch the volcano as he does. "Most important, I teach my children to meditate, to exercise their spiritual power, so they will be better in tune with the nature around them," Darto told a reporter.[1]

When I read this story, I thought of how closely my wife has watched the children, and how well she has learned to read their signs. She is as constant in her attention as Darto is, and has special connections with their mysteries, and is as alert to anything that might threaten them. Mothers and babies pay attention to each other in ways of which they are not even conscious. Their bodies communicate even after birth.

Coincidentally, the same newspaper that introduced Darto to the world also ran a story about recently discovered advantages of breast-feeding that have nothing to do with the nutritional analysis of milk but everything to do with this kind of attentive communication. For example, researchers think a baby may learn what foods to eat by tasting their variety in mother's milk, whose flavor changes with mother's diet. A baby also acquires antibodies from breast-feeding mother's milk. Perhaps because of such communication, breast-fed babies seem less vulnerable to allergies and diabetes, even to some cancers.[2]

Breast-feeding and homeschooling have something in common. Most homeschooling women that we know opted for breast-feeding. In fact, the difficulty of breast-feeding while working for a bank led one mother to quit her job with Citi-corp, stay at home with her children, and eventually choose homeschooling. The technological apparatus of breast pumps, and the apparent accommodation of nursing rooms in some offices do not bridge the communication breach between a working mother and her distant baby. In order for the baby to enjoy all the advantages of breast-feeding, the mother must hold the baby and pay close, even automatic and unconscious, attention. It's not difficult to imagine communication between the mother and baby occurring in many ways, still undiscovered and unmeasured by researchers.

Certainly a special closeness develops between the stay-at-home breast-feeding mother and her baby. She may watch the baby as closely as Darto watches the volcano. She gives herself completely to this watchful attention. For many mothers, this relationship naturally grows into homeschooling. It is probably not a coincidence that the rising interest in Lamaze births and breast-feeding in the 1980s was followed by a surge in the homeschooling movement. Many homeschooling mothers, used to spending time with their children, do not feel that they are making the greater sacrifice by leaving the workforce to stay with their children. A much more painful sacrifice would be to break the relationship that has developed between mother and child, and that continues to benefit the child physically, mentally, emotionally, and even spiritually.

As parents, we have a clear and singular objective: to do the best we can for our children. Even if the objectives of the schools were as clear and singular as our own, even if they aimed only and wholeheartedly to provide the best possible education for every single child, they could not do it. It is impossible for a school to develop the intimacy of communication that grows between a mother and her child. For schools, "the best possible" could mean only the best possible within the constraints that govern them.

A Matter of Focus

Although the contemporary school system seems to offer little of value to us or to our children, we do value the example of idealistic educators who drowned in the waves of social control and social efficiency a century ago. We agree with the humanist Charles W. Eliot that the development of reasoning power and the ability to express thoughts clearly is a fundamental purpose of education, and share his rejection of the notion that the main purpose should be job preparation. We agree with William Heard Kilpatrick that education should be "be considered as life itself and not as a mere preparation for later living."[3] We have much in common with John Dewey's experimental school, where children practiced cooking, carpentry, and candlemaking. The purpose was not to train cooks, carpenters, and candlemakers; each of these activities was an opportunity to learn subject matter such as arithmetic or chemistry in the context of a broader learning experience that also included learning to plan, learning to work collaboratively, and so forth.

Professor Clayton Christensen of the Harvard Business School coined the phrase "disruptive innovation" to describe how inventive but apparently insignificant businesses operat-

ing far from the mainstream could suddenly eclipse major corporations. Homeschooling is clearly a kind of disruptive innovation, and could replace schools much as personal computers
have replaced mainframes. The Institute of Education Sciences of the U.S. Department of Education estimated that
there were 1.1 million students being homeschooled in 2003,
approximately 2 percent of the American student population.
Yet the number is continuing to grow as families discover that
they can not only do without schools, but in fact do better than
schools precisely by doing without schools. Homeschoolers
have a different strategic focus from that of schools. Homeschoolers in general focus much more intensively on each
child's needs and abilities than do schools or teachers.

Schools cannot have this sharp a focus on the child. After
all, schools must respond to political pressures from various
interest groups, to economic pressures from teachers' unions
on the one hand and taxpayers on the other, to regulatory
mandates such as the No Child Left Behind program, and to
other forces. Schools have such a diversity of conflicting
mandates and objectives that they cannot have a single focus.

But homeschoolers can have a single focus. The success
of homeschoolers may depend on the kind of unmeasurable
communication that occurs between a breast-feeding mother
and her baby. Something happens in a homeschooling family
merely by virtue of the fact that parents dedicate time and attention to their children. The very fact that they give their
time communicates something to the children. Some of this
communication is certainly unconscious. It is a matter of parents giving themselves to their children, and their children

accepting the gift, as naturally as a newborn baby accepts the gift of its mother's breast.

Recently, some parents have attempted to provide the benefits of homeschooling to their children through hiring tutors.[4] In this arrangement some of the benefits are lost, particularly those that occur only where parents genuinely make the gift of themselves. While the students could benefit from individual instruction, customized courses, and flexible scheduling, as the most affluent always have done with tutors, they lack the particular emotional reinforcement that homeschooling mothers have been able to give their children.

The Wise Crowd

We are not exactly representative of homeschoolers, but then no homeschooler is really representative of the others. One of the strengths of the homeschooling movement is its diversity. The success of homeschooling—success by many measures—demonstrates an idea that James Surowiecki explored in *The Wisdom of Crowds:* "The idea of the wisdom of crowds also takes decentralization as a given and a good, since it implies that if you set a crowd of self-interested, independent people to work in a decentralized way on the same problem, instead of trying to direct their efforts from the top down, their collective solution is likely to be better than any other solution you can come up with."[5]

Surowiecki marshals plenty of anecdotal evidence. At a livestock fair in England, a crowd of people guessed the weight

(continued)

of an ox, and although the individual guesses were often wide of the mark, the crowd's average guess was almost exactly right. Similarly, when a submarine was lost at sea, the average of a crowd's guesses of its location was almost spot-on. When the right conditions apply, crowds of nonexperts can be remarkably astute problem solvers. For homeschoolers, the problem is education. They come to this problem with the three elements that Surowiecki identifies as most necessary to forming a wise crowd: diversity, independence, and decentralization. Their average performance beats that of the experts in the school system.

As we wrote this book, we were surprised by a reminder of how thorough and effective this unspoken communication can be. Readers with experience in business are probably familiar with the process of drafting vision or mission statements. This is a fundamental first step for any enterprise or project. We never drafted a statement of vision or mission for our homeschooling enterprise. In fact, we did not begin with a clear vision, mission, and plan. We began by groping in the dark, taking what steps we could, and groping some more. Eventually, we managed to grope toward some light, and looking back at the trail we had made we could see where we had come from and where we had arrived.

We had a vision and a mission, but implicitly. We did not really begin to think about our homeschooling enterprise in terms of vision and mission and attempt to make them explicit until we began to write this book—after we'd been homeschooling for twelve years and seen three daughters through grade school and high school and into college. In fact, we did not really think in businesslike terms of vision, mission, and strategy until near the end of the writing process, when we began to understand at last what we had done and realized that it could be put in these terms, and that these terms might help some readers get a clearer idea of what was involved. Yet while our vision and mission were implicit, no one was unaware of them. The vision and mission grew naturally out of values that were very explicit, and that we often discussed, and that guided all of our decisions, major or minor. After Martine and I had discussed the idea of vision and mission for a day or two, we decided to ask our children what they thought the objective and purpose of our homeschooling enterprise had been. They used terms almost identical to those we had been using in our private conversations. Apparently our implicit vision and mission had been thoroughly and clearly communicated to all concerned.

- -

Vision

- -

By vision we mean our vision of education.

Our vision of education is: the way of living by which children can become who they are.[6]

Every child is a person, and every person is an end in himself or herself, never a means to an end. So the purpose of a child is not to ensure that a school will stay open, that teachers will have something to do, that the society will benefit from a well-trained workforce. Our children do not exist so that we will

(continued)

have something to brag about, nor are their setbacks our failures. We must detach our egos from the children to loose ourselves in order to help them and to lessen the burden on them.

Because the child is not a means to an end, education is for the child, not for anything else. The purpose of education is to turn a child's potential into reality. Another word for this is "actualization." Education is not study, and not a manner of learning to read or write or do math or get good grades or take tests, even though these may be a part of education, if they are a part of life. It's not something you have to "get" to "get" a job. Education is living and learning and developing.

We want our children to become who they are—and a developed person is, above all, free. But freedom as we define it doesn't mean doing what you want. Freedom means the ability to make choices that are good for you. It is the power to choose to become what you are capable of becoming, to develop your unique potential by making choices that turn possibility into reality. It is the ability to make choices that actualize you. As often as not, maybe more often than not, this kind of freedom means doing what you do not want, doing what is uncomfortable or tiring or boring or annoying. Think of "going for the burn" in a weight room.

This is a countercultural vision, of course, and is not the sort of thing you find taught in schools. As we mentioned earlier, two of our daughters attended a local public high school for a semester to try it out. One of them, Lena, still talks with something like horror of a lunchtime conversation with several AP literature classmates. One of the students happened to notice her reading *The Autobiography of Frederick Douglass* and asked her who he was. She explained that he had been a slave, had taught himself to read, escaped slavery, and become a leader in the abolition movement. Another student at the table said, "I really don't understand. It would be better to be a slave if you were well fed than to be free and have to find your own food." Lena said after she returned home from her sojourn in the public schools, "Those kids *are* slaves, really. Instead of making their own decisions, they're fed by teachers."

An extreme example? Admittedly, it sounds shocking to compare schoolchildren to slaves. But before dismissing the analogy as absurdly far-fetched, consider the extent to which schoolchildren are bought and sold to benefit those with an economic interest in the school system. Bidders take a straightforward economic interest in schoolchildren, and schools sell their children in several ways.

Agency Risk

Schools sell the attention of children to advertisers, for example. In one notorious case in Georgia, a school even suspended a student for refusing to help advance a Coca-Cola advertising campaign.[7] More commonly, schools sell, to market researchers, information about students, sometimes including such personal information as names, addresses, and telephone numbers.[8] Schools also help soft-drink and junk-food makers reach children, even as they pare away physical education programs to cut costs.[9] "Many schools, particularly high schools and middle schools, generated substantial revenues through competitive food sales in 2003–2004," the Government Accountability Office reported in September, 2005.[10]

Schoolteachers certainly have an economic interest in schoolchildren, and schools, like corporations, seem to suffer from a form of agency risk. Agency risk describes the degree to which the self-interest of those controlling an institution becomes more important than the interests of those whom the institution purportedly serves. Enron, WorldCom, and Tyco exemplified agency risk in the corporate sector at the debut of this twenty-first century. The scandals surrounding these companies came about because managers put their self-interest ahead of the interests of shareholders and other stakeholders. But agency risk happens in schools, too.

Professor Caroline Hoxby, Harvard College professor and Allie S. Freed Professor of Economics at Harvard University, examined the fact that school productivity has fallen even as spending on schools has increased, and found that teachers' unions have been responsible for both. Where unions are strong, spending is higher and productivity is lower. Hoxby finds that the teachers benefit from the increased spending, but the students suffer. That's because the productivity decline is so much greater than the spending increase that students have lost, rather than gained, despite the additional spending.[11]

Politics, academic standards, and financial incentives converged to pervert and impoverish education through the No Child Left Behind program. The program aimed to address the sort of problem that Professor Hoxby identified, in which spending on schools did not improve student performance. Under this program, schools could make or lose money, depending on how well students scored on tests.[12] As a result, many teachers focused their whole educational effort on ensuring that their students pass the tests.

James Popham, professor emeritus at the University of California, Los Angeles, and an expert on tests, says that the tests are often a poor measure of both student achievement and teacher performance. Yet with school rankings and money at stake, "Teachers in desperation do things that are harmful to kids. They focus on test preparation drills they think will help, but those just teach kids to pass the test," Popham says.[13] Other strategies include barring students from taking anything except reading and math (no history, music, or science) to improve their scores on reading and math tests. "Thousands of schools across the nation are responding to the reading and math testing requirements laid out in No Child Left Behind, President Bush's signature education law, by reducing class time spent on other subjects and, for some low-proficiency students, eliminating it," the *New York Times* reported in March 2006.[14] Spending all their time cramming for tests doesn't mean that these low-performing students will improve their performance, much less that they will receive a good or balanced education.

On the contrary, to judge from our own experience, and that of other homeschoolers we know, studying things other than reading and math can be the best way to learn reading

Mission

The mission, as we conceive it, is how we make the vision come true. Our vision of education is, as we said above, the manner of living by which our children become what they are, become fully free and actualized. With this vision, home-schooling is the only way to go, because no other educational option available to us advances that vision. Our mission, then, became homeschooling, but homeschooling with a particular emphasis on freedom and on the present moment. Martine calls it "Carpe diem," Latin for "Seize the day," a phrase coined by the Roman poet Horace:

Dum loquimur fugerit invida aetas. Carpe diem quam minimum credula postero.
While we speak, odious time flies. Pluck the day, trust little in tomorrow. (*Odes* I, 11.8–9)

The phrase also describes a school of English poetry that gave us such lines as:

Gather ye rosebuds while ye may, old time is still a flying, and the same flower that blooms today, tomorrow will be dying. (Robert Herrick, "To the Virgins, to Make Much of Time")

and math. Even looking out the window can be a good way to learn reading and math, if you pay close attention and use the teachable moment. Popham says, "You in the homeschool world will be pursuing education in a well-rounded manner, and counterparts in public schools will be on the short end of a test-based instructional regimen—so you'll be even better. We're shortchanging all those kids in public schools."[15]

I have said that we see education as life itself, not mere preparation for some later state of life. But we believe that life itself is the act of a free choice repeated, repeated, repeated in every present moment. What choice? The choice to live.

The choice must be made in the present moment, because one can only be alive in the present moment. Those who are not completely in the present moment, who are distracted by the future or the past, worried about tomorrow or about yesterday, are in a sense not living.

But the present moment must be chosen. Those who do not choose are also in a sense not living. When we light up because we can't quit, or don't stick to an exercise program, or get into yet another destructive relationship even though we know better, or fester resentfully in a dehumanizing job because we're afraid to quit, or do anything that undermines our freedom to choose, we undermine our humanity.

It is as though every present moment offers us an opportunity to choose to live freely or not. Habits, attitudes, and circumstances may constrain our choice, making us more or less free. Every time we repeat an act, we reinforce a habit, so the stronger a bad habit is, the less free we are. Education is largely a matter of learning to form the right habits, the good ones, those that make us stronger and freer instead of weaker and less free. That is what we mean by developing virtue.

A Child's Freedom

We want the children to be virtuous. The virtuous don't deny nature, but they certainly control nature, as any gardener does. We balance control with freedom. We try from the beginning to be open to the children, to listen to them, to work with their natural gifts, and not just to superimpose a curriculum or be authoritarian about what they have to learn. If God gave us free will, we are in no position to take freedom away from children. Following the child's nature can be something as simple as finding a book the child likes to read instead of taking the text or the curriculum the authorities have said is good. It can mean following the child's interest in history even if it means jumping around a bit. That makes it harder for us in a way as homeschoolers, but in the long run I think it gives us more satisfaction as educators and parents.

Martine

CHAPTER FIVE TAKEAWAYS

✓ We value the example of idealistic educators such as humanist Charles W. Eliot and William Heard Kilpatrick, whose ideas drowned in the waves of social control and social efficiency a century ago.

✓ Something happens in a homeschooling family merely by virtue of the fact that parents dedicate time and attention to their children.

✓ Diversity, independence, and decentralization make homeschoolers as a group extremely effective at finding the best way to accomplish the educational mission. To borrow a phrase from author James Surowiecki, they are a "wise crowd."

✓ Our vision of education is: the way of living by which children can become who they are.

✓ Our mission is homeschooling with a particular emphasis on freedom and on the present moment.

✓ Every present moment offers us an opportunity to choose to live freely or not. The choice must be made in the present moment, because one can only be alive in the present moment.

— — — — — —

SIX

Just Go:
Travel as Homeschooling

f it hadn't been for the bomb, we'd never have met.

The bomb was on the tracks somewhere between Rome and Pompeii. An assignment had taken me to St. Gallen, Switzerland, and then to Rome. My son Billy had joined me. We came down into Italy by train, on a sunny May afternoon, over blue Swiss lakes and through the Alps. Our first stop was Florence. At the Institute and Museum of the History of Science there, Billy and a docent demonstrated the law of constant acceleration of falling bodies by rolling a ball down a polished and beautifully inlaid inclined plane dating from about the time of Galileo.

A pendulum swings back and forth as the ball rolls, and at each complete oscillation of the pendulum the ball strikes one of the several small bells set along the plane. It was remarkable to see how greatly aesthetics seemed to matter to the old master, whose telescope and compass were not only instruments to serve science but objects of art in themselves, lovely in the details of their craftsmanship. We toured the Uffizi Gallery, and while viewing the surviving Botticellis, we heard about the bonfires of Savonarola on which the fervent Botticelli had burned his own work before renouncing painting as a worldly vanity. We attended mass in the Duomo, where we saw religious art as the painters and sculptors meant it to be seen, not as something warehoused in museums but as a pointer toward a living mystery. We visited Michelangelo's workshop, with its centerpiece, the *David,* and a photographic mural showing tourists looking at the *David,* and so we looked not only at the *David* but also at the people around us looking at the *David.*

We noted with interest how the experience of the museum, with its docents and crowds, was distinct from the experience of the art in the museum, and the experience of the art in a museum distinct from the experience of the art in a church, and the experience of art in a church visited for a liturgy distinct from the experience of art in a church visited in order just to see the church and the art. You don't have to study phenomenology to begin to grasp the fundamentals of experience. You just need to pay close attention—and Billy was taking everything in.

This is all homeschooling, though it's not home and it's not school. Travel, as opposed to tourism, puts things in a new light, and I think what we saw in Florence did that for Billy. I'd like to say it deepened his understanding not only of history but also of struggles over faith and science and art that still occur today, though in different contexts. But that might be a stretch. After all, we were only in Florence for a short time, just long enough to include it in his neighborhood, to make it a place that in a sense belongs to him now. Maybe that's enough. I do know from some things he's said that Renaissance history and art aren't abstractions anymore because he's experienced them, literally touched them, so they're part of his own life. What he makes of that will be up to him.

We then came to Rome by slow evening train. Billy started a conversation with a young Italian couple as we rode, and by the time we arrived they'd given us their e-mail addresses and phone numbers and insisted that we get in touch so that they could show us around the city. We didn't take them up on the offer, though I'm sure they would have been happy to do that. We had already planned a full itinerary.

We made it a point to visit the Vatican Museums first, arriving early in the morning, before the tour groups. The assignment that took us to Europe had come at the height of the tourist season, and soon a crowd extruded through the museum corridors like paste through a nozzle. Viewed from above it would have been the same hue as paste, a blur of shades of gray. The tourists were disproportionately elderly and retired. Of course, the Europeans tend to take their vacations all at once, in August, so most of those with jobs were at them in May, and schools were also still in session there, as in the United States. Even so, with Rome so close to the rest of Europe, so easy to visit, the absence of other young people surprised us. Instead of eager and curious youth, there was only a parade of adults who were taking the trip of a life-time, the one that they had looked forward to for years, maybe for decades, and finally decided to take "while we're still able." But the young also need to travel, because they will have a lifetime to profit from what they learn, and a life-time to deepen their learning by traveling well.

We hurried to the Sistine Chapel, where we watched *The Last Judgment* as if it were a movie, noticing the motion in it and the suspense. We talked about the story behind each ceiling fresco, looked from every angle, trying to see. The tour groups, which of course had to get everything, including shopping, into a tight schedule, came, spent their fifteen minutes in the chapel, and then rushed off. The chapel was a base to touch, and they'd touched it. We were touching base too, I suppose, but we lingered, spent an hour on the *Judgment* and another hour on the ceiling, and still felt we were rushing through. Two hours wasn't enough time to learn to see the Sistine Chapel, and two years probably wouldn't be either, and maybe twenty years wouldn't be. But in order to learn to see it, we had to learn to see other things too— the Belvedere Apollo, for example, whose torso provided the model for the *Last Judgment*'s Christ. So we moved on too.

Seeing is something we learn to do. I wanted Billy to learn to see as much as possible, and thought that in order to do so he should have at least an impression of the sweep of Egypt and Greece and Rome and Gothic and Renaissance. That way he could store memories that would help him make new connections and perhaps learn to see everything (people, buildings, history, faith, science, music, everything from masterpieces of art to fast-food franchises on the Interstate back home, by everything I mean everything) in a new and richer context. So we made our own path through the galleries, seizing the opportunities that presented themselves, sometimes listening to two or three tour guides at once, and comparing their presentations, which on the whole were a dog's breakfast of artsy trivia.

Senator Daniel Patrick Moynihan once said that everyone is entitled to his own opinion but not to his own facts. That would probably sound radically strange here, where every guide seemed to have a proprietary set of facts, and some just made theirs up—especially one fellow American, wearing a backwards baseball cap and a guide badge, who showed to my satisfaction that what we-the-people lack in history we make up for in creative and barefaced bamboozling. The people in his group seemed to think they were getting their money's worth, because they hadn't heard any of this stuff from other guides. From time to time Billy tugged my sleeve. I was delighted to see him growing more cautious and skeptical about what he heard, especially when he heard it from someone in apparent authority. I think that is fundamental to a good education. And if it comes back to bite me from time to time, that's a price worth paying.

The Bomb and the Bilker

The bomb mattered because there wasn't enough time in a day to see all we hoped to see in the Vatican Museums. We planned to come back early the next morning, but were delayed by the run-up to a public transport strike that broke out during our visit. Instead of being in line around six A.M. we didn't arrive until almost seven, by which time the line had already stretched for blocks and was getting longer with every step we took to reach the end of it. There would be at least a two-hour wait, and that seemed a real waste of time, so we changed our plans. Billy had been talking about the ruins of Pompeii before we left home, and two hours is about how much time it takes to travel from Rome to Pompeii, so we took the underground back to Stazione Termini and saw on the schedule that we could take a midmorning train and arrive in Pompeii around noon. That gave us plenty of time to go back to our hotel, conveniently near the station, and chow down at the complimentary breakfast buffet we had skipped to arrive early at the Vatican. We made a couple of sandwiches for the road, and then crossed back to the station to buy the tickets.

The line was unbelievably short, and I, at least, was feeling as if I'd managed things brilliantly. Everything was going to fall into place. I got up to the ticket window in no time and gave the agent the number of the train we wanted. She was wearing the gray, expressionless face of a bored functionary until I did so. Then she looked at me with empathetic disappointment, pursing her lips and shaking her head as she explained that the train would not be leaving because they had found a bomb on the track. "All the trains are canceled," she said, her disappointment deepening and getting more animated as she noticed my son's disappointment. "It would be better for you if you were to go another day." We conferred and pondered and eventually decided to take the underground toward Ostia for the beaches.

Well, a day or two later we heard the trains were running. We bought a ticket for the earliest departure of the day, and after we were under way found out that the bomb was still on the track. We found out because although the train had gone at nearly normal speed for a half hour or so, it made an inexplicable stop in the middle of nowhere, sat on the tracks awhile, and then rolled away from the stop in extreme slow motion. The air conditioner went out. The conductor sat down on the floor in the passage between the cars, hung his legs out the open door, and smoked pensively as he watched the scenery crawl.

Someone sitting across the aisle from us passed over a copy of the *International Herald Tribune*. A short item informed us that the bomb was a World War II artifact uncovered during construction. Efforts were still being made to remove it. The British air force had gotten involved somehow, because they had dropped the bomb in the first place. We heard on the passenger grapevine that trains had to be rerouted to detour around the bomb, and although we were miles and miles and miles from the bomb, we were moving slowly because every train in southern Italy was creeping through the detours. We would later learn that the bomb had become a tourist attraction in its own right, with people driving out to look at the work going on to remove it. So it was causing some traffic jams, too. All of this gave us plenty of time to gaze at vineyards and castles en route, and by the time we arrived in Pompeii, it was so late that we wondered whether we'd be able to find and get into the ruins.

This made us easy prey for the white-haired cabdriver with a face that could have come out of the Who's Who of Gangland. He came up to us as we were checking our map before walking to the ruins, and knew his business well enough to tell us immediately that the ruins were far away, that the gates were about to close, and that if we didn't go right now, by cab (there were no other cabs at the station but his at this late hour), we couldn't possibly get in. We more than suspected this was a lie. One look at his face and you would have to suspect anything he said would be a lie. Lying had shaped it in a way that is difficult to describe but impossible to miss when you see it. We were equally sure, even though we had never been to Pompeii and didn't know anything about the cab fares, that the rate he told us he'd offer as a special favor because we were Americans and his son lived in New York was extortion. But even a mediocre success of a liar knows enough to mix some truth into what he says, and this guy looked like an accomplished prevaricator, so at least some of what he was saying was probably true, and we had no way of knowing which part that was.

We had a brochure for the ruins, but we knew that the hours printed in our brochure might be as irrelevant as those printed on the train schedule had been. So we got in the cab. The driver sensed our suspicion and tried to beat it down with a fire-hose blast of fast talk in broken English, from which we learned, among other things, that when Senator Ted Kennedy had come to Pompeii to visit the ruins he had ridden in this very cab. Just in case we didn't understand, the driver slapped the seat forcefully and repeatedly, shouting, "*Kennedy! Right here!*" When we failed to react with duly credulous awe, he indignantly shoved his hand behind the visor and pulled out a sheaf of papers, shouted some more, waved them emphatically, and thrust them back at us. They were letters of reference and recommendation. The one we had time to skim praised his excellent and very reasonably priced services, and concluded with the signature of a doctor with a Park Avenue, New York, address.

The driver grunted as we read as if that ought to show us, by God, how wrong we had been to doubt him. A glance showed that the style was so effusive and Italianate that it must have been the product of a son or nephew with schoolboy English and access to a computer and printer. But we didn't have time for more than a glance before the old cheat tried to deliver us to a restaurant just outside the gateway to the ruins, where he insisted that we should have lunch before beginning our tour. We reminded him that he'd said the gates were about to close, whereupon he waved his hand as if we were crazy, and told us how wonderful the pizza was at this restaurant, and reminded us that all Americans like pizza, and how important it was to eat before the tour, because there would be nowhere to eat once past the gate. We nodded agreeably and put the agreed gouge for cab fare into his hand as he talked, and walked away toward the gate, as his expostulations grew louder and more multifarious. All in all, we considered the money well spent.

Being bilked by a southern Italian cabdriver of his quality

and credentials was an invaluable lesson for life. Billy has often alluded to him subsequently in the context of conversations about advertising offers and even political campaigns here in the United States.

We spent a few hours wandering through the city destroyed by erupting Vesuvius, overhearing several tour guides as we went. We hadn't done much homework on Pompeii, and hadn't been expecting the nondescript brick warren of buildings whose function was unapparent until a guide explained it—and then, of course, it always could have been possible the guide was making it all up. No matter that all of history has to be made up by somebody, otherwise there'd be no story in it at all. To tell the truth, though, we weren't all that interested in the buildings. We had a morbid interest in seeing the so-called plaster mummies, those famous casts of people caught in one ordinary moment of their daily lives over two thousand years ago that happened to be the moment of their deaths.

They hadn't expected Vesuvius to erupt. It was just a mountain to them. It hadn't behaved like a volcano for so long that its crater cradled forests in which the Spartacus slave revolutionaries had hidden. Towns clustered at its base. Then, surprise! Vesuvius sent poison gas and lava down. The eruption simultaneously killed and immortalized, encasing people of Pompeii in ash that turned to rock quickly enough to capture their expressions as they died. That rock was like molds from which the bodies melted away in time like lost wax. In the nineteenth century, archaeologists began to fill the molds with plaster to get casts of the bodies. The casts show that sudden death had not been painless in Pompeii. You can see by their positions how they struggled to do two contradictory things: on the one hand they struggled not to breathe the poison in the air, and on the other they struggled to breathe air. Although some of the casts were away on tour with a special traveling exhibition, there were enough under glass around Pompeii to send our minds bungee jumping between the stoic contemplation of mortality and the spectator's thrill at the piteous special effects Vesuvius had engineered.

Having seen the dead, we had a lunch at the restaurant on the grounds (the cabdriver had apparently been mistaken about the absence of food in the ruins) and watched the living for a while. Archaeologists were still excavating Pompeii, and we hung over a fence looking at sun-browned professors and graduate students dig and sift, dig and sift, putting together more pieces of their story. We looked over the bay at Vesuvius, not too obscured by smog that day, wondered a little apprehensively whether it might have a surprise in store for us, and then walked back to the train station. It was an easy walk.

Sharing, Borrowing, Adapting

The bomb, of course, was still a factor. We caught one train and rode a little while and then caught another, and eventually arrived in Naples, and after some trouble with our tickets because of the delay, did find our way to the platform. That's where we met the Latimers—and if it had not been for the bomb, as I said, we would not have met them. They were Americans and we were Americans and we struck up a conversation as we waited, wondering whether we were on the right platform, and in the course of figuring out that we were on the right platform we found out that we were all homeschoolers. Their children, already in college, were not with them, but when we mentioned that Billy was the fourth of our children to come to Italy in their early teens, we found ourselves on common ground.

Mr. Latimer enthusiastically endorsed the idea that travel was an important part of homeschooling. In fact, he said that they had even sent their children to live for a while with relatives in Italy, to experience the difference in cultures, learn the language, and so forth. We found out that they had an eclectic approach similar to our own. For example, we found that we had the same attitude toward television, a disposition to keep it at a safe distance. Mrs. Latimer said that the first decision she made with respect to homeschooling was to get rid of the television. We have kept ours, but use it very selectively. We also found that our eclecticism put us in a curious position with respect to homeschool groups and organizations. Mrs. Latimer talked about being in the odd position of both fitting in and not fitting in with most groups she joined. She said she was in groups that had nothing in common with one another beside the fact that she was in them; but she found that she had something in common with the people in each, and so she had often been a sort of bridge between groups. We knew that feeling.

Then the train rushed in, and we separated to go to our

seats. A couple of days later, we met them again, at the Vatican Museums, where they had a good spot at the front of the line and let us cut in. Mrs. Latimer was for no particular reason wearing a *bindi*. She had converted to Catholicism years before and was not Indian, but she had spent some time in India, and brightly said she wore the Hindu forehead decoration just because she liked it. Why not? I shrugged, the museum doors opened, and we parted ways.

Mrs. Latimer's remarks about bridging two homeschooling movements stayed with me, though. She had said that the fact that people homeschool doesn't really mean that they have anything in common, because homeschooling means so many different things. I understood what she was getting at but wondered whether that was quite correct. I was thinking about this when Billy and I took a turn into a little-frequented gallery, the Pio museum of early Christian funerary art. Decorating the fourth-century sarcophagi on exhibit there are relief carvings, mainly scenes from the Bible and from pagan mythology. I don't mean that some sarcophagi have Bible carvings and others pagan carvings, as though the dead were fighting culture wars even in the grave. No, the Christians themselves tapped paganism to decorate their sepulchers. The earliest Christians were clearly catholic that way—small *c*—what the Merriam-Webster dictionary calls "broad in sympathies, tastes, or interests." So the image of the Trinity appears alongside the Roman goddess Juno, and together on a sarcophagus lid, they bless the memory of a Christian's wedding. Elsewhere, the image of Jesus as a good shepherd resembles a pagan Roman image of the shepherd as a symbol of philanthropy. I thought of Mrs. Latimer, clearly Catholic, wearing a Hindu *bindi*, at home in both evangelical Christian and secular homeschooling groups, sharing, borrowing, adapting, and it seemed that she had antecedents in ancient Rome.

The Strangeness of the Expected

Travel is important education. Yet our most educational travel experiences have been the spontaneous, unexpected trips for some ordinary purpose. We hardly ever go anywhere just for the sake of traveling, never take tours, and almost never do field trips with homeschool groups. When I have a business reason to be somewhere, we seize the opportunity to turn a business trip into a family trip, and every family trip is somehow educational because of how we travel. We travel the same way when we plan holiday visits to grandparents, or when there's a wedding or a funeral to attend. The way we travel is with our eyes open to see it all, because wherever we happen to find ourselves is invariably a destination by definition, if only because we arrive there. So we can even travel without leaving home.

Only once have we gone on a regular, all-American vacation. That was when Uncle Jim, who had struck it rich in the Texas oil patch, decided to invite the whole family— grandparents, in-laws, and cousins included—to a Caribbean cruise on the Big Red Boat and a visit to Disney World. It was a grand gesture, a Texas-sized invitation, and of course we appreciated it and enjoyed everything immensely, and remember it to this day, because the children look back on it as one of the more surreal experiences of their traveling homeschool life. They learned what they would never have believed, that there are people who pay steeply to go where everything that happens will happen on schedule, where no experience will have rough surfaces or sharp edges, where nothing will be too hot or too cold even for a moment, where even the exotic food won't taste too different from what you're used to, where you can't get lost even if you want to because someone is looking out for you, where there won't be any detours or surprises, and where there will never be the slightest risk. There may be fireworks and parades, but they'll happen right on time and exactly where everyone knows they'll happen. Everything will be in perfect order, even the simulacrum of adventure in Frontierland, a land of no stray bullets, no stray dogs, no horseflies, no horse manure, no sweat, no dirt, no splinters, no frowns, and no hard words or hard feelings, where everyone smiles all the time and even the outlaws are polite and helpful if you ask them a question.

It was all so strange.

Nobody's Tour

Our way of traveling is admittedly eccentric, and our spontaneity sometimes as shocking to others as the planned and scheduled is to us. Other homeschoolers, hearing on the grapevine that we take the children to Italy every three or four years, sometimes ask Martine what "program" we use. They seem to think that the normal way of traveling is to become part of some formal, organized tour group. When she answers that we don't use a program, we just go when we can go, people seem somewhat bewildered. I had a similar exchange with an Asian homeschooler when I happened to mention a trip that we had taken. She asked, "Oh, how do you do that? My son always wanted to go to Alaska and Canada because he was very interested in nature but I didn't know how to go." I found that hard to understand and said, "You can fly to Alaska for fifty dollars sometimes if you watch the airlines and catch a price war right. You can take a train. You can drive. You just do it."

Yet our way of traveling is our way of living. We are constantly traveling, even when we are standing still. We see our lives as a movement from one present moment to another. Each moment is a time and place we are passing through and will never pass through again. Each moment is precious and unique. We never know what the next will be, and any plans we make are merely provisional. We want to experience each moment as fully as possible, and we want the same for the children. We don't put our travel in the hands of tour organizers for the same reason that we don't put their education in the hands of schoolteachers. Discovery should be part of education, and of travel, but it is seldom part of tours or schools.

We aren't dogmatically opposed to tours, though, and now and again we make an exception to our rule about not joining tours. The National Park Service offers a walking tour of the Freedom Trail in Boston, for example. It's a good introduction and worthwhile, especially if you have only a day to spend in Boston. Sometimes, too, we'll even plan to go to a reenactment, like the one that occurs around the anniversary of Paul Revere's ride. Such reenactments are usually almost pro bono efforts by a local historical society, but they're as interesting to us for what they say about today's America as for what they say about history. The fact that people meticulously assemble historical costumes and spend their free time lending color to patriotic celebrations, maybe get a small stipend, but far from enough to cover their expenses, is somehow something good about America.

But these are minor exceptions. By and large, we just go. The value of just going is that you go to places you would never plan to go to, where there doesn't seem to be any reason to go, where even if you ask the people who live there they'll tell you there's nothing much to see. But that's because so many people close their eyes to things around them. So few know how to travel without going away. There are places that any local with an exit leaves to go somewhere interesting, somewhere exciting. There are places where kids say, "There's nothing to do," and where adults sink themselves in debt to go somewhere really exciting on their vacations, maybe Disney World, for example. But when we get to those places people are aching to leave, those places with nothing to see or do, we find plenty. We learn things there that we'd never learn by going to a place all set up to entertain and educate us. We learn these things because there are no professional guides to take us around and show us everything they think we should have planned to see. We learn these things because we're on our own, bumping into random facts of life.

One such trip took us in the Christmas season on a grand circuit of Atlanta, Georgia; Winston-Salem, North Carolina; Paducah, Kentucky; St. Louis, Missouri; Chicago, Illinois; Cincinnati, Ohio; Sharpsville, Pennsylvania; then back to New Jersey. The trip came about because I had to do some interviews for a project and the interviews had to be face-to-face with people in some of those cities. But since it was Christmas season we decided to include family visits to grandparents in St. Louis and Ohio.

We normally travel on a very tight budget, because, as I mentioned earlier, our family of eight gets by on one unsteady income. Gas prices were pretty low in the late 1990s, when this trip came up, so we drove. Martine and Bridget stayed up all night before we went, making food to take along. When you hit the American road with a bunch of children, finding good, nourishing food can be a problem. Town after town offers the same overpriced fast food, too fried and too salted, from the same familiar chains. So we usually take something homemade that keeps well, is easy to handle without too much mess in the car, and is nourishing and tasty and a bit out of the ordinary for us. One time, that meant spicy meat pies. Another trip, it was Chinese tsung tse (a sort of sticky rice dumpling stuffed with bits of meat, bean curd, spices, nuts, mushrooms, or whatever you want to stuff it with, wrapped in bamboo leaves and steamed). We also packed our dog-eared copy of Jane and Michael Stern's *Roadfood* and a book called *Food Finds,* by Allison Engel and Margaret Engel. (Now we can consult the first on the Web, but the Web wasn't the Web back then.) Both of these books listed good local restaurants or food specialties region by region. America, even in this age of commodification and fast-food chains, has plenty of spots where people are making some unique candy or cookie or foodstuff that they sometimes don't make on a very big scale, and even in this day of online commerce, sometimes don't distribute very far, so you have to go there to get it.

Those places aren't often on the interstate. One of Bridget's favorite memories is of the time we drove fifty miles out of our way to visit the Ridgewood Barbecue on Old Highway 19E in Bluff City, Tennessee. We got lost in some parts of Tennessee we would never have had any reason to see if we hadn't gone looking for the Ridgewood and gotten lost. "Lost" isn't really the right word, though, because every place we go becomes our destination when we arrive. It's getting off the main road, and wandering around the back roads through unplanned detours, that opens our eyes to the country. There's a lot to be said for wondering and straying from the highway. Yes, that's spelled correctly: I mean wondering what's off the highway, wondering what's next, wondering why, or just plain wondering at what's before our eyes now. We've driven back roads through the Upper Peninsula of Michigan, and the Cornish pasty we discovered there taught us more than any book could about the Cornwall miners who settled in the area, who used to cook them on their shovels when the ore was rich. The ones we had were enormous, gut-busting stews of potatoes and meat, all rolled in a crust.

Of course the mines aren't what they used to be anymore, and the money isn't either, and now the pasties are specialty items instead of a workingman's staple food. The money pulls out, leaving the holes behind. We've driven through abandoned factory towns in Pennsylvania and North Carolina, passing acres and acres of rusting buildings or crumbling brick warehouses, seeing firsthand the urban fossils left by "creative destruction," that phrase of Joseph Schumpeter's that so benignly describes the wrenching forces of economic progress in a competitive market. Lena still remembers two barefoot children in torn T-shirts who watched us with big, incredulous eyes as we rolled through their Kentucky holler on one of our detours a decade ago. "I was surprised to see such poverty in our country," she says, of children who were about her own age then.

Accidents and Incidentals

It seems that the memorable things about our trips are always the accidents and incidentals. We spent the night in a no-name Maryland motel by a cornfield, where in the middle of the night a drunk drove up the long driveway, apparently under the misimpression that he was still on the highway, and crashed through the lobby window, totaling a couple of cars along the way. When we went to Atlanta, Martine and the children visited numerous excellent museums while I went about my job. More vividly than any of these, they remember then six-year-old Yankee fan Billy, riding the Atlanta subway, talking baseball with some mullet-haired Braves fans in denim shirts and work boots, who were carrying their lunchboxes and still smarting a little over the Braves' defeat by the Yankees in that year's series. Billy rubbed a little salt in but everyone took it all in good humor.

In Winston-Salem, North Carolina, I interviewed an evangelical Christian auto dealer who was trying to sell cars according to Gospel values, and then, instead of going to the famous art museum, we toured the RJReynolds cigarette factory at Whitaker Park and saw a collection of materials on tobacco and tobacco advertising and learned about tobacco auctions and growing tobacco. Although we wouldn't usually travel to a city just for them, we never ignore industrial museums and factory tours, because they tell you something about the people of a place, about the local economy, and often a lot about wider history.

If nothing else, when you go through a factory you see how things come to be, and see machines that exist to do things the necessity for which may never have occurred to you. Tobacco was such an enormous part of American history and culture and especially of Southern history and culture that it would be a poor education that ignored it. The same logic took us to the Coca-Cola museum in Atlanta, bourbon distilleries in Kentucky, and a cheese factory in Wisconsin. In

Chicago, we visited the Mercantile Exchange, and watched the currency-futures traders shouting and flailing in the pits, and I tried to explain what they were doing and why. It may not have been clear to the children, but it's often not clear to the traders themselves. At least they understand that there is such a place, and it affects everything that has anything to do with money, and much that has to do with power.

We do visit historic sites when they lie on our road, but what the children remember is mainly what they absorb about the gradations and contrasts of America. There's a kind of learning that can only come from moving through the landscape, from traversing the mountain barrier that penned the country along the coast until Daniel Boone blazed a trail through, that comes from seeing mountains and smoking mist in the morning and then knowing why the only name for them can be the Smokies. So much of history depends on place, depends on the river or the mountain pass or the rich or the poor earth. You can read in books about the westward push of pioneers seeking land, but that's not at all the same as coming from a stretch of sandy, rocky, or red clay soil to suddenly see the deep, flat, black earth of the bottomland. Camping alongside Lake Michigan, the children swam and found that as soon as their heads came above water, mosquitoes surrounded them. So they ran back to the tent pursued by a black cloud of little bloodsuckers, and then listened to the mosquitoes scream against the side of the tent.

We crossed the Mackinac Bridge at Sault Ste. Marie, where the subject of mosquitoes came up when I asked for directions at the tourist information station. The lady at the desk said the bear hunters had been doing "real good" that year because the mosquitoes were pushing the bear out of the deep woods into the open, where they could get a clear shot. It's one thing to read about the voyageurs and another thing to move along those rivers and lakes getting bitten by mosquitoes as they may have been bitten by mosquitoes, to heft a reproduction of their enormous canoes and learn the consequences of the birch absorbing water, and understand why a big cause of death among the voyageurs was hernia, and then to ponder the New France they thought they were building.

You can learn a lot about history without deliberately studying it, just by driving through places where it happened. You learn things from seeing that you can't learn from reading. Our eccentric travels showed us the ruins of lost civilizations, such as the one that erected vast burial mounds near Cahokia, Illinois, and used, somehow, a calendar of wooden poles as sophisticated in its astronomy as Stonehenge, but who vanished from their vast and populous city before Columbus made landfall in the New World.

We learned by our detours that every American age bequeathed to posterity a heritage and portion of lost cities, places that grew up for some reason or another and for a brief while were centers of power and wealth or even of Kingdom Come itself, like Nauvoo, Illinois, a utopia of the Mormons, then a utopia of the Icarians, and then merely utopia, whose Greek roots mean "nowhere." America is full of dreams and the ghosts of dreams haunt her, gibbering like birds along brushy stretches of road or river where the only memorial of their ever having lived may be a worn historical marker or perhaps a local mall named after a vanished city.

After the 2004 presidential election, Bridget was talking with some of her college friends in the Northeast, passionately frustrated Democrats who were trying to understand the defeat of their favorite. One of them said that anyone who looked at the map of red and blue states could see that the blue states had all the best universities, so they probably had the smartest people too. It was a moment when she saw how provincial sophisticates might be. Having traveled to the red heart of red states, she knew the variety of the country in a way that her friends did not. She'd found out something about the contrasts in America by driving from states where billboards promote casinos and lotteries to states where billboards ask if you're saved, and where towering trios of crosses top roadside hills, and where there are more churches than bars. She'd been in places where, because she was a Catholic, she was not a Christian as far as the locals were concerned, though she'd been hearing the Bible read in church since before she could read it herself.

She recognized, when she was listening to her friends assuage their defeat with the ointment of snobbery, that they had never seen Paducah, Kentucky, or Sikeston, Missouri, and that until they did they'd never really get it at all—no one can explain it and you can't know until you see it.

When we travel, we take tapes or CDs. Good music is as hard to find on the road as good food, and we haven't found a guide to do for local radio what the Sterns and the Engels did for local food. So we pack a box of music and history and literature. On one trip we listened to the complete *Odyssey*; on another trip, *The Three Musketeers* and *The Scarlet Pimpernel*; on another, the Teaching Company's course on Winston Churchill. But we mix it up, with selections of music and history, old radio shows, and readings from novels or poetry, and of course when we can find good local radio we tune in. There is less and less of that to be found as radio consolidation imposes uniform playlists and categories of programming throughout the country, and even the shows and so-called noncommercial sponsorship announcements on public radio start to sound the same everywhere.

But despite these preparations, it's the accidents and the incidentals that make a trip educational. It was a flush year when we took the girls to Chicago and left the boys with Grandma and Grandpa for two or three days in December. They saw an exhibit of Degas at the Art Institute, and saw the Museum of Science and Industry, but what they really remember is how to walk when the wind is blowing in the Windy City, how to keep your back to it and how to use buildings to break it, and that the city (or someone) put ropes along the curb so pedestrians could catch themselves and not be blown into traffic.

We made our way through Canada going to places we hadn't planned to go, and finding surprising reasons to be there. Driving across Ontario we suddenly saw a sign that said "Shrine of the Martyrs," so we pulled off to see what it was. We found a church and memorial to the French fathers, on the site of their mission to the Hurons, with the skull of

Jean de Brébeuf, smashed by a tomahawk, and near the door piles of crutches left by people apparently miraculously cured.

We just go. Even our trips to Italy have depended on the unexpected. Bridget and I first started the tradition one year when someone called and asked if I could give a talk at a conference in Venice, because I had just published a book on a subject related to the conference. Ordinarily the invitation would have been for me and my wife, but we were closing on a house and packing to move and couldn't leave the children on their own, so Bridget went with me instead. When we arrived at the airport, we were bumped from our overbooked flight, given two vouchers in compensation, and put on another flight. (The compensatory vouchers provided tickets for Martine and the twins a year later, just after the 9/11 attacks, when airlines were desperate for travelers to fly.) While I did my job, Bridget toured the secret gardens of Venice with a contessa who was showing spouses of conference participants around, and the conference banquet in a palazzo on the Grand Canal was, she conceded, a reasonable way to celebrate her fifteenth birthday. A few years later, another assignment took me to Switzerland, to the campus of the University of St. Gallen, and that time I brought my then fourteen-year-old son Billy along, as discussed earlier. While I worked he was on his own on the campus, but we had the evenings, and afterward we had a long train ride through the Alps together, and then Italy. We didn't have deep, cinematic conversations or so-called quality father-son moments. We were just together, spending time together, doing what we might ordinarily do but doing it in an extraordinary place. When we travel anywhere, we are together being there, and that is sometimes the most important part of the experience.

When we have a chance and half an excuse to go, we go. It's easier than many people seem to think. We rarely join tourist groups but once, when Bridget and I were in Rome for just a couple of days and didn't want to spend hours queuing at the Vatican Museums, we bought a slot on a tour to get into the museums quickly. We let the guide show us to the Sistine Chapel, then let the tour group leave to go shopping without us while we explored the museums together. Otherwise, we rely on chance and circumstance. The principles we follow in travel are the same principles we follow in the rest of our education.

Serendipity and randomness are the best reasons to go anywhere, because you can never plan in advance to discover the things you don't know. If you know them in advance, then you don't need to discover them. We hadn't thought in advance about the Corpus Christi feast that closed everything in the Vatican one day in Rome, but Billy and I went early to the square of St. John Lateran, and attended the papal mass, and joined the procession, carrying candles through the narrow streets all the way to the Basilica of Santa Maria Maggiore. He, dodging ahead, walked almost immediately behind the great white-and-gold car on which the pope knelt in adoration of the Eucharist, itself white in the center of a sunburst gold monstrance. We could not have planned for this, because we did not have any idea what we might have planned for.

When the surprise of a trip comes up, we make few preparations. We may pack a few CDs or take a book, possibly a guide to local restaurants, and we look ahead to economize on hotels. If we have to, we can always take a tent. The important thing is to go. And surprise is the best reason to go. But you may not have to go to go. Wherever you happen to be, there you are. All you have to do is open your eyes and you travel into a new state—the state of awareness.

CHAPTER SIX TAKEAWAYS

✓ Travel, as opposed to tourism, puts things in a new light.

✓ We travel to Italy to include it in the neighborhood. Renaissance history and art aren't abstractions anymore.

✓ We want our children to store memories and make connections that will help them see everything in a new and richer way.

✓ Our most educational travel experiences have been the spontaneous, unexpected trips for some ordinary purpose.

✓ It seems that the memorable things about our trips are always the accidents and incidentals.

✓ Industrial museums and factory tours can tell you something about the people of a place, the local economy, and wider history.

✓ You can learn a lot about history just by driving through places where it happened.

✓ Serendipity and randomness are the best reasons to go anywhere, because you can never plan in advance to discover the things you don't know.

✓ Wherever you happen to be, there you are.

––––––––

SEVEN

Taste and See:
Family Dinner as Homeschooling

One of our daughters recently joined several friends in an informal discussion to help other homeschoolers prepare for college. A homeschooling mother had organized the evening, a very casual get-together with about a dozen mothers and children around a dining room table. Someone asked a question about curriculum and testing and Bridget laughed.

"Daddy would ask us a question, and if no one knew the answer, we had to finish our meal before we could go look it up," she said. "We'd all hurry to finish." For the very young ones, the question might be, "Wherever I look, I see south. Where am I?" As they grew older, it might be, "I went into the backyard and started digging and dug so long that I came out on the other side of the earth. Am I at the same latitude or the same longitude? What is the closest big city?" Some of the questions asked about history, or biography, or astronomy, or oceans and rivers. The point wasn't to ask for something that the children knew but to send them to look up facts they didn't know. There was a lot of lively guesswork, and they learned that there are two kinds of knowledge: knowing something, and knowing how to find it out. Most important, though, they learned how to laugh together whether their answers were right or wrong. It was a game, after all.

Our daughter reminded us, when she remembered that game, of how much our curriculum depended on food, on cooking together, and on eating together. We usually eat three meals together each day, and those meals have been central to our homeschooling. In fact, table talk became one of the most important forms of learning for us, easily as important as reading. Reading and conversation blended, one reinforcing and stimulating the other. We played word games and talked and read Dickens at the dinner table, but that wasn't all. A meal brought history and geography and poetry and music with it. Let's take a walk through our kitchen now, to show you all that went into our meals.

The World in a Kitchen

Here in the corner by the south-facing window is a metal baker's rack holding various kitchen stores and equipment and paraphernalia. For example, here's a three-liter tin of Greek Horio olive oil that George, an AT&T retiree we know from the dojo, told us about several years ago. The children went with us to the Greek store in Kenilworth to buy it, and at that store they also found out about islands where thyme grows wild and so abundantly that bees make honey out of it, and the Greek store sells this thyme honey in small, amphora-shaped glass bottles, and it tastes very different from any other honey. They learned about the different kinds of anchovies packed in oil, and about dozens of cheeses—the goat cheese soaked in wine, the soft and hard sheep cheeses, and the domestic and imported feta cheeses—and about kalamata olives, and green olives stuffed with garlic or blue cheese, and black olives cured and shriveled. Lena taught herself to make baklava, using honey and orange water and phyllo and walnuts, and it's better than what we can buy. It's not unusual, when we eat these Greek foods, for the children to remember something they read of the Greek myths, or to remember the long road trip several years ago when we listened to the new translation of the *Odyssey* on tape.

We're dipping good bread in great olive oil, snacking on cheese, maybe on the side the pepper dip Martine figured out how to make after tasting the dip the Greek store sells (good, but hers is better). Maybe we're just talking about how the price of cheese has gone up and a child asks why and we explain the floating relationship between the euro and the dollar, illustrating with examples from their recent Pokémon trades. The mention of Pokémon reminds someone else of a graphic novel or an anime, and another conversation launches and could go anywhere through history or literature or current events. So education comes with the meal, and is something the family does together, like eating.

But back to the kitchen, back to the baker's rack, with its can of Japanese sesame oil, its wok, its ice shaver, and their implicit lessons in geography that a conversation makes explicit in good time, and the big colander we use mainly for Italian pasta or Chinese noodles, or the bread machine, a gift redolent of the Midwest—a geography with its own comforting cuisine—and a deep fryer used mainly to fry fish, when we catch them ourselves, usually when Grandpa comes to visit from Missouri. On the central island in the middle of the kitchen is a rack of random spices, curry powders from the Indian stores in Iselin, New Jersey, where we once found ourselves accidentally joining a motorcade for a wedding led by a white coach and white horses that passed into a drive where a hundred girls in blood-red saris threw rose petals.

There are dried fruits from the Asia Food Center, and a half-bottle of Madeira left over from the stew we made last week, and a few of the ceramic bowls Lena made in a course she took at the community college as part of her homeschooled high school curriculum. There's a box of English breakfast tea. Our pediatrician suggested we start the boys' school day with a cup of tea to help them focus—they may have some mild symptoms of ADD and she opposes drugging children as much as we do, but a little caffeine in tea might help, she said.

Cookbooks

Of course, there are the cookbooks. Too many cookbooks, if it were possible to have too many cookbooks. They've overflowed the capacity of the kitchen bookshelf, though it's a six-foot-tall, three-foot-wide bookshelf discarded from an office. Some of the books are stacked one atop the other six deep, some lie along the top of rows of other books conventionally shelved. Several are falling apart. The shelves bend under their weight. I have to do something about that sometime. But the kitchen seems to be the most reasonable place to keep cookbooks and food history books, even though some have to be kept in boxes on the floor alongside the shelf.

The thing is, we use these cookbooks fairly frequently. We never know when the idea will come up to cook something Burmese, and we need to have the cookbook, which Martine purchased in Rangoon in 1982, there just in case. But you can't cook something Burmese without mentioning something about Burma, without someone talking about George Orwell, or quoting Kipling's "Mandalay," or reminiscing about our friend Mo, a Burmese Buddhist who seems eternally imperturbable. Mo, who used to run a small computer shop in town with his brother, an activist opposing the dictatorship in Myanmar, sometimes drops by as suddenly and astonishingly as enlightenment itself, with his moon-broad face and beatific smile and penumbra of peace. An unexpected knock on the door and there he is: Bodhisattva Mo, whose mindful eye saw through the illusion of bugs and viruses and bad drives and who in his compassion got our system up and running again and whose idea of cashing in a chit was to ask us how he might publicize some rally—a favor not for himself but for the cause of freedom and the sake of others. Of course, we have to talk then at dinner about politics and activism and history and freedom, about religion and philosophy, or maybe just about why every country seems to have its own kind of rice, why this Thai jasmine rice or that Japanese Kokuho Rose tastes not at all like the other, and what makes this sweet rice so sticky.

Do I digress? So much of our homeschooling is digression that digression sometimes seems to be the whole point of it. So much depends on people dropping by, dropping in, showing up, so much depends on unexpected encounters with surprising nuggets of wisdom carried by people we haven't seen for years, or never expected to meet, or would have ignored on the street if not for something, some tap on the shoulder or upside the head.

There are Burmese and Chinese and pan-Asian cookbooks, Latin American and French and Italian cookbooks. There's Elizabeth David's oeuvre, nearly complete, and a big set of old Time-Life books on food, and a few other random books collected over the years, like most of our books, from various used-book sales. There's a Jamaican cookbook I brought back from an assignment on an aquaculture project in Jamaica, helping sell technology for raising freshwater shrimp and tilapia, when my employer was an Israeli arms dealer and my office mate was one of the fellows who had gone to Tehran with Ollie North to get the Iran-Contra trade under way. The Jamaican client was a born-again Christian who owned a chicken-processing operation and a lot of acres studded with ponds, and between the ponds were, here and there, airplanes that had crashed, and he said that the drug dealers kept trying to use his property against his will to launch and land, but it was obvious that sometimes the landings could be rough. Big black vultures with red heads winged low over the ponds.

The cookbook has lasted decades longer than the job. I keep telling myself I'm going to try that recipe for cowfoot and beans someday, but haven't gotten around to it yet. Next to it is Cy Littlebee's cookbook, published by the Missouri Conservation Commission, with recipes for every kind of game and near-game from beaver to venison, including even possum and skunk. Next to it, or nearby, soul food cookbooks and a few books on Latin American cooking, the *Joy of Cooking* with its revelations about a lost era of Americana, when Jell-O was new and fashionable, and some cookbooks, long out of print, published by the *Farm Journal,* that Martine has had since she was growing up and going to 4-H Club and entering recipes in county fairs in her rural Ohio childhood. The cookbook shelf could support courses in geography, history, pop culture, and science. In fact, it has. Harold McGee's *On Food and Cooking* was one daughter's gateway into chemistry and science.

In the pantry, if you happened to be the kind of house-guest who opened doors of medicine cabinets and pantries to peek, you'd find a similarly heterogeneous aggregation of oddities and contradictions, and every one has some kind of story or other, and every one has some kind of homeschooling application or other. The instant mashed potatoes are mostly for thickening soups or for topping shepherd's pies, and that's about all we know about English cuisine except for roast beef and Yorkshire pudding, if you don't count the home-brewed stout and ales we used to make when there seemed to be less work and more time. The Hamburger Helper figured inevitably in a discussion of economics and budgeting, but it's remark-able what a variety of cuisines you can sample on a budget if you shop carefully and do it yourself. There's a bottle of Cam-pari that Billy and I brought back from our trip to Italy last year. But here's a tin of coconut juice and on top of it a tin of water chestnuts and alongside it cans of sardines and cans of smoked oysters—for a while, smoked oysters were the only food that Blaise would dependably eat (we stocked up at $1.29 a tin). There's maple syrup—a friend in Ohio makes maple syrup, and we've talked at dinner about tapping trees and boiling sap.

In the refrigerator, there is a partial pot of soup, soup be-ing an important economizer for a one-income family, but so tasty that we can almost look forward more to the soup than to the ham or the turkey or the beef roast that gives us the soup bones in the first place. There's Chinese dried black beans, chopped garlic, vitamins, tahini sauce, horseradish sauce, chestnut spread, jams, orange juice, lemon and lime juice, oyster sauce, a block of Parmesan cheese. Seasonally, there will be homemade candied orange peel, representing a holi-day tradition in the family for at least two generations now. In every jar or bottle, there's a conversation, a route into golden realms.

Ora et Labora

Family meals and family conversations are ways to teach and learn. This bourbon fudge from Gethsemane Abbey in Kentucky reminds us of a trip we took there as a family in 1996, and of the Benedictine tradition of prayer and work and holy poverty that has such resonance for us. Prayer is central for the monks, but so is work—it is also a kind of prayer, or an expression of prayer. The prior of the abbey, Brother Raphael, said that in prayer you make promises to God, and in work you deliver on them.

I have probably told too often at our table, when we discussed some atrocity or headline-grabbing crime, the story of Brother Raphael, tall and lean, with a fringe of white hair, on his eightieth birthday, out on the green lawn beyond the cloister wall. He had been living in the monastery then for over fifty years. For the first decade or so, he said, the Trappists still maintained strict silence, and if while they were working in the fields near the road a car went by, someone gave a warning and the monks turned their backs to the road in order to avoid temptation from what they might see—a woman, perhaps. The discipline was less arduous now, and Brother Raphael was wearing civilian clothes, a work shirt and a baseball cap. Birds were making noise all around us. I asked him what he had learned after all of those years in the monastery, and he said, "I have learned that whatever I read about in the paper, I could do. You know, you pick up a paper, and you see some guy going to jail for something, maybe he killed somebody, or robbed somebody. I could have done that. If it hadn't been for the advantages I had, the advantage of a good family, or the right mentor, or the right person to say something at the right time—that could have been me. I'm no better, no different." Brother Raphael's insight has added some perspective when the table conversation turns to justice. I have not talked with him since long before the terrorist attacks of 9/11, but I doubt that he has changed his mind.

Another interesting gift of the monks to us was their attitude to work. At a time when the business of the monastery was taking off, and monks were working eight or ten hours a day, they took a vote and decided to cut the hours back to just the amount of work necessary to pay the bills. They had a franchise that could have become big business, a kind of Famous Amos in a cowl, but they didn't want that. They needed money—to an extent—but they needed time too, and they insisted on balance. Balance also prevented them from taking another course: that of licensing their name and brand to a commercial business and getting out of work altogether. Work was valuable for its own sake, was its own kind of prayer, as indispensable as the chapel.

These memories and principles are not peripheral or tangential to our homeschooling curriculum. Education is not just about learning facts and techniques. It's about learning a way of life. Would it be a digression to mention here Mother Teresa and her sisters, Sister Assumpta and Sister Margaret Joseph and Sister Lourdes and the rest, who came into our lives about the time that we began to homeschool? To discuss our homeschooling curriculum without mentioning them would be to lie by omission. They moved into what had been an abandoned convent near the church in Plainfield mentioned earlier. When you live on one inconstant income in a marginal city, it helps to have the example of the Missionaries of Charity. It is not that they are poor but that they are joyful because and by means of being poor. They are a sign of contradiction to a society that regards poverty to be a punishment for laziness, instead of a virtue and a blessing. Martine was closer to the sisters than she would take credit for being. Several times we were able to meet Mother Teresa, who blessed every one of the children—blessing the last *in utero* in 1997. It's no digression to say that the teaching of Mother Teresa and the example of her sisters was core curriculum for our homeschool.

The teaching is not one you can read—what you can read is only the shell of it. The teaching is the fact of a woman in a white sari with blue stripes along the edge, who owns nothing, who flew planes in the Caribbean before she joined the convent, or was a nurse, or a teacher, or a wife and mother or widow, who is walking down a ghetto street in the sunshine, alongside another similar woman in similar robes, and they don't even own the shoes they wear, because their poverty is complete, yet both of them smile with a depth of joy you never see in photographs of stars or socialites, because (not despite but because) of complete poverty. They taught us how to live and some taught us how to die: Sister Mary Shawn, Sister Cabrini, knowing they would die, accepting that they would die, smiling. Part of our homeschool curriculum was to go to the convent that afternoon and see Sister Mary Shawn, or what she had left behind, in a plain pale pine box, cotton stopping ears and nose, unembalmed, ready for a prompt burial. No, it's no digression. This was part of our curriculum.

To rely on a saint for an example is not to do exactly what a saint has done. As we see it, education means grasping the spirit of the saints, and living it in the distinct circumstances of the present moment. We are not religious contemplatives, do not go barefoot or abstain from meat or rely on charity for our support. But the following, adapted from *Ascent of Mount Carmel*, Chapter XIII, by Saint John of the Cross, hangs on a bookshelf here:

ALWAYS STRIVE TO CHOOSE

The hardest instead of the easiest
The unpleasant instead of the pleasant
The least instead of the most
The worst instead of the best
To desire nothing instead of any desire . . .

We find that those words summarize succinctly and usefully what practice is necessary for an education that aims at becoming fully free and fully human. It is not necessary to understand very much about Carmelite spirituality, or about the mystical night of the senses and the night of the spirit, before following this advice. In fact, very probably, all the understanding that really matters comes in time to those who follow this advice faithfully.

Monks and nuns have preserved important wisdom about living. It's not in what they say but in their living. Although we are not monks or nuns, that wisdom seasons our life—and our education. But you have to know how to see it and always be looking, because it is easy to miss. This is part of homeschooling too: learning to pay attention.

Here in the dining room are two small photographs framed in gray, twisted twigs—Anna and Lena at a Chinese music camp sponsored by the Buddhist Light International Association on its Deer Park complex in upstate New York. They are sitting on the veranda of the Buddha Hall looking over the Catskills, Anna playing the *erhu,* a sort of Chinese violin, and Lena the *dizi,* the Chinese bamboo flute. The pictures were taken the week after Lena and I had spent a week following a shaven-headed Chan master, a Buddhist nun in a brown habit, who led us along the paths through the woods, by the lake, near the rushing water, up the hill to the Buddha Hall, teaching us to pay attention to every breath and every thought.

The Way

We are Catholic homeschoolers and we are catholic homeschoolers. We are not Buddhists unless it is true that everyone who tries to pay close attention and be mindful is thus by definition Buddhist. Yet the Buddhists tell us that we are Buddha, as the whole world is Buddha, though we do not clearly see our Buddha nature. And part of being Catholic is to be catholic: to accept what is true regardless of its source. This catholicity was no innovation of the Second Vatican Council. The great Thomist Josef Pieper quoted the Taoist sage Lao-tse in *The Silence of St. Thomas,* introducing his chapter on the saint's negative element with the sage's aphorism that "the Name that can be pronounced is not the Eternal Name." Saint Thomas Aquinas himself had reached out to the then-suspect Aristotle for useful techniques of arriving at truth. And Buddhists have preserved certain skills and dispositions and techniques of cultivating attention that are useful. On this principle of catholicity, the Zen and Taoist masters contribute to our core curriculum. What matters is not so much reading as practice.

It is central to our homeschooling approach, this conviction that the truth we pursue may be vaguely suggested in what we read or hear, but is only really found in the vivid present moment. Truth is a relationship, not a doctrine but rather a being in relationship. We find truth by living it, not by studying it.

The Chinese Taoist philosopher Chuang-tzu tells of a wheelmaker who saw a duke reading the sages, and commented that he was reading "scum." The duke replied that the wheelmaker would die if he couldn't explain that comment satisfactorily. The wheelmaker explained that the secret to making a wheel was to know how to cut. Cut too fast, and the cut would not be deep enough. Cut too slowly, and it would not be steady enough. Hearing or reading about this was almost useless, though. Knowing how to balance fast and slow, deep and steady was something that came only from experience. He could not even tell his own son the secret, and he supposed the same was true of the sages—everything really necessary and useful to know had died with them, and the rest, the scum, remained in books. The wheelmaker lived.

The understanding of what it really means to be human is similarly elusive, because in order to have it one must live it. If you live it, you don't need words; if you don't live it, words can perversely obscure rather than clarify it, make it harder rather than easier to grasp. Our words are, at best, a vague map. Like any map, they may be useful for a while, and even their vagueness may be useful, as a reminder not to place too much confidence in the map. The risk of a good, clear map is that we may put too much focus on the map and fail to see what is all around us.

There is a famous story about a monk who prepares to pass the examination on the question the master had given him and after lengthy meditation and contemplation goes in to the master confident he has the answer to the question at last. The master looks at him and asks, "When you came in the door was the umbrella on the right or left of the sandals?" The monk has not paid attention; he bows and leaves knowing that he's failed. That Zen story captures the spirit of homeschooling, at least our homeschooling.

Education is life itself, not just preparation for later living. Life is a pop quiz, a trick question. You see people everywhere preparing for what they thought was going to be the question, only to be surprised by what they had not noticed. We've met scores of the thousands who prepared to pass what they thought would be the test by building a career at AT&T or Lucent or some other big, supposedly safe employer. They thought that the test question was, "Can you keep your head down and make steady progress through the corporate ranks?" But the test question really was, "Can you jump nimbly when the foundations fall out from under you?"

We feel that this is the most important teaching that we can give our children, yet we cannot give it to them. We can only hope to show it to them in our own living, and trust them to discover it in theirs.

It is a core principle of our homeschool curriculum that the conventional and commonly accepted version of anything is probably an illusion and possibly a lie, including the things that school boards and teachers and fellow parents all take for granted, accept unquestioningly, and unthinkingly reinforce for one another. Many things that everyone takes for granted make sense only when you exercise no skepticism and pay no attention, but it's easy to get swept away by the herd. To see things as they are, to trust your intuition, you have to observe closely things and yourself. To trust your own instincts you have to have a breadth of experience and input and exposure you get only by leaving the herd behind. To believe that foundations everyone trusts can crumble, and to be ready to jump if they do, you need to know that other foundations everyone trusted have crumbled before, but you only find out by resisting the security of numbers and looking where the "safe" can't see.

CHAPTER SEVEN TAKEAWAYS

✓ Education comes with the meal and is something the family does together, like eating.

✓ So much of our homeschooling is digression that digression sometimes seems to be the whole point of it.

✓ Education is not just about learning facts and techniques. It's about learning a way of life. Trappist monks showed us how to balance the need for money against the need for time. Mother Teresa's Missionaries of Charity taught us the joy of poverty.

✓ What monks and nuns have to teach is not in what they say but in their living.

✓ Part of being Catholic is to be catholic, to accept what is useful and true regardless of its source. On this principle of catholicity, the Zen and Taoist masters contribute to our core curriculum.

✓ If you don't live it, words can perversely obscure rather than clarify it.

✓ Life is a pop quiz, a trick question.

- - - - - - - -

EIGHT

Homeschool Groups:
Building a New System

Go to the ant, O sluggard; consider her ways, and be wise.
Without having any chief, officer or ruler,
she prepares her food in summer, and gathers her sustenance in harvest.

(REVISED STANDARD VERSION, PROVERBS 6:6-8)

When people mention the scriptures in the context of science these days, they are often talking about conflicts between the two. So it may come as a surprise to learn that the above words of the Bible are perfectly in agreement with the discoveries of recent scientific research. When it comes to ants, the writer of the Book of Proverbs clearly knew his business. Ants indeed have no chief, officer, or ruler. An ant queen makes no decisions, and there are no ant generals or CEOs giving orders. "The basic mystery about ant colonies is that there is no management," writes ant researcher and Stanford professor Deborah Gordon. "Each ant scratches and prods its way through the tiny world of its immediate surroundings. Ants meet each other, separate, go about their business. Somehow these small events create a pattern that drives the coordinated behavior of colonies."[1]

The brief and apparently insignificant meetings of ants are in fact ponderously consequential. No individual ant amounts to much, yet an order emerges from each ant's and all ants' efforts. Ant colonies solve complex and challenging organizational problems. They optimize the number of workers performing tasks such as foraging for food, nest maintenance, and caring for young, and the number on each task changes as needs change. Ants move from cleanup duty to nest maintenance when the nest needs work, from nest maintenance to foraging when an abundance of food demands more foragers. No one tells them to. They just do it.

Researchers studying systems and organizations have lately begun to pay close attention to ants. They have also discovered other contexts in which small, undirected, apparently random meetings of particles, insects, or even people result in vast and orderly patterns powerful enough to change the world. No one really understands how it happens—that's what makes the study so interesting, of course—but no one can doubt that it happens. The evidence is right in front of our eyes, wherever we are. "The essence of emergence is this sense of much coming from little," writes John H. Holland, a founding father of complex system and nonlinear science. "We are everywhere confronted with emergence in complex adaptive systems—ant colonies, networks of neurons, the immune system, the Internet, and the global economy, to name a few—where the behavior of the whole is much more complex than the behavior of the parts."[2]

In each of these examples, unplanned, local, and completely free events give rise to large, stable, yet powerfully adaptive systems. Something like emergence is at work in the way cities organize themselves when planners don't get in the way.[3] The late activist for and student of cities Jane Jacobs wrote that the apparent disorder of a city gives rise to "a complex order . . . all composed of movement and change."[4]

Manchester, England, is one of the great examples. The city arose as an unregulated area where tradesmen of various sorts practiced their crafts without the approval or oversight of municipal authorities. Manchester had no city government, yet Friedrich Engels saw systematic precision in its organization. Systems don't have to be controlled from above to be stable, powerful, and effective. In fact, the most successful systems aren't controlled from above. As one contemporary journalist observes, "You don't need regulations and city planners deliberately creating these structures. All you need are thousands of individuals and a few simple rules of interaction."[5]

Homeschooling is such a system. It's unplanned and uncontrolled. It is a system built from the bottom up by thousands upon thousands of individuals making free choices about education. Yet these free choices somehow give rise to educational communities that are as stable and distinctive as the city neighborhoods that Jacobs studied, and that achieve results, as we have seen, measurably superior to those of conventional education systems.

Homeschoolers freely choose to associate with one another, and they form real, personal relationships, one by one. Yet although they are pursuing their own individual, freely chosen objectives, homeschoolers everywhere in the country seem to come together in similar ways.

That's the essence of emergence. Emergent systems create patterns of order from apparently random events.

There is a common and mistaken stereotype of homeschooling that envisions a mother and a child, or several children, working alone, isolated from the community. This stereotype makes it easy to imagine that homeschooled children are unsociable and unsocialized. But homeschooling is intensely social. In fact, because homeschoolers are not bound by the constraints of districts and school boards, they can associate much more widely, spontaneously, and creatively than the conventionally schooled.

Some years ago, the phrase "social capital" entered our language to describe the value created by such intangible elements as trust, reciprocity, communication, and community. In his seminal book *Bowling Alone,* Robert D. Putnam explains, "Just as a screwdriver (physical capital) or a college education (human capital) can increase productivity (both human and collective), so too social contacts affect the productivity of individuals and groups."[6] Putnam's book described the erosion of social capital in America, and cited as evidence the declining participation in bowling leagues, churches, civic and political organizations, and volunteer groups.

But the homeschooling system goes very much against the trend that Putnam identified. Homeschooling has all the virtues of the wagon train or the pioneer settlement. Home-schoolers pitch in, volunteer, carry their fair share, help one another, and succeed together. Wherever there is homeschool-ing, there are homeschool groups and networks. These groups have a lot in common no matter where they are—and are at their best where regulations don't put a damper on their cre-ativity and initiative. Putnam concluded his book writing, "In the end, institutional reform will not work—indeed, it will not happen—unless you and I, along with our fellow citizens, become reconnected with our friends and neighbors."[7] That happens in homeschooling, perhaps to a greater degree than in any other American phenomenon—and certainly to a greater degree than in the conventional schools.

Like ants, homeschoolers are constantly absorbing infor-mation from their environments, noticing and responding to needs as the needs occur, and feeding information to one an-other about what seems to work to meet those needs. They form groups easily when the need arises and break them up easily to form new groups in response to changed needs. Only groups that meet some needs better than any known alternative can long endure. By this kind of unmanaged, un-coordinated, somewhat chaotic, and unpredictable activity, without any chief or leader, and with no financial assistance from government (in fact, sometimes while fighting off at-tempts by the government to make their activities illegal, and almost always while paying a sort of financial penalty in the form of taxes to support public schools they don't use) home-schoolers have achieved educational results measurably su-perior to those of schools, and across more than one scale.

From the unmanaged initiative of homeschoolers, a parallel educational system has emerged, one with results much more impressive than those of the public school system, and by and large even superior to private schools.

As mentioned earlier, studies consistently find that when it comes to academic achievement as measured by standardized tests, homeschooled children beat schoolchildren hands down. On tests where the average performance of public school students is at the 50th percentile, the homeschoolers average between the 65th and 80th percentile.[8] The fact that the homeschooled excel academically may not come as news to many readers. But there seems to be a widespread and false impression that homeschoolers have to sacrifice a social life to achieve that level of excellence. This false impression is so common that even some college admissions officers who are unfamiliar with homeschooling occasionally mention it as a possible concern.

So it may be surprising news to many that homeschooled children are more sociable and better adjusted psychologically than the conventionally schooled, according to numerous research studies. In 2000, the *Peabody Journal of Education* published an issue focusing on homeschooling, noting that "research on the academic achievement and social adjustment of homeschooled children abounds," and that "research studies indicate that homeschooled students perform well in terms of both academic achievement and social and psychological development."[9] Researchers have reported that the homeschooled participate in more extracurricular activities,[10] have a more diverse range of social contacts,[11] and have higher scores on socialization, social maturity, living skills, and communications tests[12] than schoolchildren.

Homeschoolers have built for themselves a system that matches or surpasses the best that schools can offer, not just in the classroom but on the playing field and even on the dance floor. Barred from public school athletic teams, homeschoolers built their own teams. Then the teams became leagues, and the leagues proved competitive with the best athletes from the conventional school system. As a result, many homeschooled children have gone to college on athletic scholarships and a few have become draft picks for professional teams.

Homeschool Sports

Although some states do open their public school athletic programs to homeschoolers, most don't. In some states, homeschoolers have gone to court to gain the right to play on public school teams. Perhaps even many homeschoolers don't know that homeschooling through high school doesn't have to mean giving up the opportunity to play competitive athletics. Homeschoolers are forming their own teams and leagues, and homeschooled athletes are more than holding their own against the best that public and private schools have to offer. Chris Davis, founder of the Home School Sports Network (HSPN), says, "I'm no fan of public access. I don't think we need it."

An annual homeschool basketball tournament in Oklahoma City draws hundreds of homeschooled teams every March, from as far away as Alaska. The Homeschool World Series Association (HWSA) brings eight top teams from four homeschool baseball divisions to Florida annually. There's homeschooled football, too. In 2005, the Rocket City Cowboys won the National Christian School Athletic Association Division I championship. "Football is the most rapidly growing homeschool sport," says Davis.

The success of homeschool sports is somewhat counterintuitive. Chuck Hendricks, board member of the Dallas-Fort Worth-based Home School Athletic Association (HSAA), says, "The challenge in our organization is to organize people who have fundamentally decided that they didn't want to be organized." The HSAA nonetheless includes homeschooled baseball, basketball, volleyball, and—starting this year—football teams.

Not all homeschool athletes are outstanding, but it's not unusual for homeschooled high school athletes to go on to play in college athletics, sometimes on scholarship. A few make it to the pros. In June 2005, the Minnesota Twins drafted Matthew Betsill, a Furman University junior who had played for homeschooled teams through high school. That was the second homeschooler drafted by the pros. The first, who had played for the homeschooled Atlanta Barons, went to the New York Yankees in the mid-1990s. Barons coach Kevin Renz, formerly a scout for the Cleveland Indians, says, "I see the quality of homeschool baseball getting better each year. The talent is rising to the top and we're beginning to see where we fit in."

(continued)

Forming a homeschool team isn't hard, but finding games can be. Public schools often won't schedule games with homeschooled teams, sometimes because regulations prohibit it. Coaches of several homeschooled teams say they rely on private schools to provide the competition they need. This may require some diplomacy.

Tim Day, a public school teacher and for eighteen years a high school basketball and football coach, is a board member of both the Home School Athletic Association and the Homeschool World Series Association. He says, "Not only do you have to be competitive, but you have to be nice about it. It's okay to lose to the best teams—in fact, the preference is that we lose but lose barely, by one or two runs. If they only beat us by one or two runs they want to play us again because we're competitive, but they can save face by not being beaten by a homeschooled team. That's the best teams. The midrange teams are accustomed to getting beaten by us but they want to play us again because we're nice about it." Player-eligibility rules are also important. Day says that school teams don't want to play select teams, so the Texas HSAA has rules that restrict eligibility to homeschoolers, that allow students to play high school ball for only four years, and that make them ineligible if they graduate.

There are also many individual sports that are popular among homeschoolers of our acquaintance. Some participate in sports for recreation, others to compete and work toward technical excellence. Among these sports are martial arts (judo, karate, tae kwon do, and jujitsu, for example), skiing, swimming, tennis, golf, fencing, and archery. The lack of a homeschooled team or a welcoming school in the area need not rule out athletics for homeschoolers.

If, as the old chestnut says, love is a game, it may even be appropriate to mention homeschooled proms in this context. A homeschooled girl in our network says that the best thing about homeschooling is that she can go to a prom every year if she wants.

Systems Matter

It's not unusual to hear, especially from opponents of homeschooling, that homeschoolers would achieve the same results if they were in conventional schools—and in fact might improve the conventional schools by their presence. However, this suggestion ignores the role played in that success by the networks, groups, and trust that homeschoolers form—their social capital. Homeschooling works better because it works differently. Homeschoolers have their own organizational models and owe their success, in large part, both to the fact that, and to the way that, they organize.

The school system is an organizational legacy of the Industrial Revolution, a bequest of efficiency expert Frederick Taylor and his acolytes.[13] It's bureaucratic, vertical, inflexible, and top-down, built to resemble an efficient factory making standard products. Homeschooling, though, is more like an emergent system: self-organizing, horizontal, bottom-up, a system at home in this era of artificial intelligence, neural networks, globalization, fuzzy logic, and chaos theory.[14] It is because homeschoolers are free to come together and separate at will, to try new ways of doing things and new things to do, that homeschooling works as well as it does.

Our family experimented with several approaches to homeschooling, beginning with a rigorous curriculum, relaxing over time as we gained confidence, and eventually putting together an educational program that includes elements of several styles—and that still keeps changing. One of our consistent guiding principles has been that education must be complete, including not only academics but also athletics and music. In schools available to us, serious physical education was not available at the elementary level, and at the high schools in our area the situation wasn't much better. Team sports usually seem to provide little experience or training to any but naturally gifted athletes or those whose parents have invested heavily in extracurricular clinics and training camps. There's no reason to suspect that anything we might have done in the schools would have changed that situation.

As far as music is concerned, it tends to be one of the first programs to feel the knife when schools cut back—or change their focus to test performance. Nothing we could have done in the schools would have changed that.

With respect to academics, we mean a different thing by academics than the schools seem to mean. We think that an ideal class size is between one and twelve, and that education is best conducted in mixed-age groups, and that there are no right or wrong answers when it comes to some things, such as the way one responds to a work of literature. Our goals and priorities are clearly different from those of the school system, and we are so much in the minority that it would be quixotic at best to suppose that we could sway the system around to our way of thinking.

The fact is, parents and students face serious impediments to working within the existing school system. Institutional constraints, administrative boundaries, teacher contracts, instructional policies, and organizational inertia make it quite difficult for people in the school system to exercise freedom, initiative, and creativity, to try something, take a chance, even risk failure, in order to meet a need or solve a problem.

So we built our own system.

Our experience is fairly typical of homeschoolers we know. Even among committed Christian homeschoolers, quality of education, not religious indoctrination, is often— and increasingly—the reason to homeschool. Scratching and prodding through the tiny world of our immediate surroundings, making individual choices in response to individual needs, homeschoolers create communities, structures, and systems that protect education from the vicissitudes of school budgets, fickle pedagogical fashions, and misplaced priorities—such as putting tests and grade point averages ahead of learning. By so doing, homeschoolers protect their children not from exposure to new ideas but from lack of exposure to new ideas. The homeschool scene is much more various and innovative and free than the public school scene, and much more successful at the job of educating children.

Homeschoolers accomplish these things because they work together, like ants. No one tells them what to do. They just keep doing what seems best to them, trying and trying again, and eventually they find what works. But how do homeschoolers come together? As you might expect, they come together any way they please. Homeschool groups take different forms depending on the people in them and the reason for them.

When we first started out, we met fellow homeschoolers at the Manassas NACHE homeschooling conference, and were impressed by their enthusiasm and how much we seemed to have in common, except that none were from our geographic area. If we had enrolled in any of the curricular programs represented there, we would have been linked to nearby families with this bond. We might have looked harder for a group if we had not had both Mom and Dad at home, working together and supporting each other.

As the years wore on and our approach became more flexible, both because we grew in confidence and because the arrival of babies, book projects, and occasional bouts with the flu blasted holes in our scheduled work, we grew into some aspects of "unschooling." Occasionally we would lose our nerve. Self-doubt and stifled questions would shatter sleep. Were we kidding ourselves?

On one of our trips to the library Martine saw a notice for an "UnNet Conference," organized by Nancy Plent. We had heard of Nancy before, as had most people who were homeschooling in New Jersey by the mid-nineties. The workshops and speakers that Plent brought together at the conference, like Plent herself, were inspiring (though not in a religious way) and reassuring. It's hard to say how many people Plent's example had emboldened and encouraged, but there is no doubt that her conferences sustained our effort.

Plent was a trailblazer. She had started to homeschool in the late 1970s, before homeschooling was even a word. She and other pioneers around the United States chose to keep

---

Unschooling or Homeschooling?

For readers puzzled by the terms "unschooling" and "homeschooling," today the difference usually hinges on the degree of structure. Broadly, homeschooling is always a form of unschooling, as it does without schools.[15] Homeschoolers may dispense with textbooks, class schedules, and lesson plans in order to learn by building robots, acting in plays, raising rabbits, riding horses, or just walking and looking around. Unschoolers, on the other hand, may use some textbooks or other materials from curriculum publishers, simply because those are good tools to learn certain things they want to learn. We've done both ourselves.

At the highly organized end of the spectrum, homeschooling can mean starting the day with the Pledge of Allegiance, then moving through hourly lessons in which Mom or Dad consults a script from a curriculum company before saying anything to the children. At the other end, unschooling can mean pure, absolute laissez-faire. But whatever the merits of the extremes—and each extreme has its merits in some circumstances; otherwise no one would choose it—over time most

(continued)

homeschoolers tend to gravitate to a broad middle that gives the child a mixture of autonomy and discipline, or provides a crutch of external discipline to help the child learn to practice self-discipline. A day in the life of an unschooler may look just like a day in the life of a homeschooler. While the two terms may denote the same thing, the connotation may differ. Unschooling often connotes a secular education, so those who call themselves unschoolers may do so pointedly to emphasize that they are not religious. In fact, one sometimes hears devoutly religious homeschoolers describe what they do as "Christian unschooling" or "Catholic unschooling" to stress that though they are eclectic in their pedagogy, religion is important to them.

their children out of the school system, and for lack of a better word called what they were doing "unschooling." The emphasis was clearly on rejecting the constraints and perversity of vertically organized, rule-bound, bureaucratic schools and liberating children to be alive, alert, involved, and human. She persevered in avoiding any hint of structure or organization in founding New Jersey's Unschoolers Network.

Like many unschooling mothers, Plent always had an independent streak. "I've not set out to be different in any phase of my life," she says. "But that seems to be the way I end up anyway—maybe because my folks let me think differently and didn't stifle it. She was one of the first mothers to have natural childbirth at Jersey Shore Medical Center, and says that if her doctor hadn't agreed, she was "thinking of giving birth on the front lawn of the hospital."

Those Who Can

When the cooks refuse to eat what comes out of their own kitchen, it should probably be a warning to diners.[16] Nancy Plent was a teacher for nine years before she decided to bail out of the school system completely. That's less paradoxical than it sounds. An impressive number of teachers opt for homeschooling when they are making decisions about how to educate their own children. The leader of one homeschool group in our area recently surveyed her group's membership and found that over a third were families in which one parent either was or had been a teacher. In another homeschooling group, we met the former registrar of a public school in one of New Jersey's wealthiest districts. We know of a public school principal whose own family homeschools. It's possible that teachers and school administrators may be disproportionately represented in homeschooling because, having taught in or managed schools, they're not intimidated by the idea of teaching.

Although research studies show that teaching credentials are all but meaningless as a measure of a teacher's competence, the general public doesn't usually read such studies.[17] So in some states, regulators require credentialed teachers to supervise homeschooling programs, and even in states where there is no such requirement, a lot of people seem to think that you have to have studied education before you dare to teach. Yet teachers who turn to homeschooling know from their own experience what nonsense an education degree or teaching credentials may involve, how bad the public system really is, and how little good and how much harm school can do.

Having spent nine years teaching elementary school, Nancy Plent had quite a bit of experience from which to judge. "I hated school when I was a child, though I was teacher's pet very often," she recalls. "I had so many interesting things to do at home that school was a terrible interruption in my life. My father had a florist shop and we had dogs and a parakeet and aunts and uncles dropping by. It was a busy place and I helped with all of it. But in school I sat with my hands folded and waited forever for the kids who didn't give a hoot to finish their lessons. There was nothing to do but look into space. It was a bore." By college graduation she had so completely forgotten how much she had hated school that she became an elementary school teacher teaching third and fourth grade for nine years. She got tenure, and then threw it away. "Seeing the expressions on kids' faces made me remember. I tried to make school a good place to be, but I saw the expressions on faces of kids as they came in and finally I said, 'I don't want to do this.'"

Founding the Unschoolers Network

She visited some alternative schools in New Jersey and New York and actually worked with a friend to cofound a short-lived alternative school. "It was chaos because her ideas of freedom of education were very hippieish, and I didn't have my own ideas firmly located," Plent says. "In the alternative-school movement it was common knowledge that there would always be an October crisis. Parents would spend the summer in love and understanding and agreement, and by October somebody would say, '*That's* what you meant by "learning at his own pace"? *That's* not what *I* meant.' Nobody had an image of an alternative school that worked, except Montessori, and that was too structured."

Her son was born in 1971. Her husband, Malcolm, had grown up in the UK, and his memories of school included the occasional caning. "When we saw that little face, just born, both of us said, 'No way he's going to school!' But I didn't know how we'd accomplish it." In 1977, when her son was about the age to start school, she bit the bullet. One week she spent the grocery money to put an ad in what was then very much a counterculture publication, *Mother Earth News,* asking for advice about how to keep her child out of school legally. She got twenty responses from around the country, one of which told her to check in with John Holt, the author, educational reformer, and advocate of unschooling who had just launched a newsletter called *Growing Without Schooling.*

Nancy had read John Holt's books, but she was reluctant to call him directly. So on her birthday her husband surprised her by arranging a phone call. "I picked up the phone and a voice said, 'This is John Holt. I wanted to wish you a happy birthday.'" When she asked Holt what the laws were in New Jersey, he told her that he was hoping she could tell him. So she took on the assignment of checking the legislation and discovered that New Jersey's school laws required either school attendance or equivalent instruction elsewhere. Although there was no requirement that she communicate with the school at all about her educational plans, she sent a letter to the principal, saying that she would not be sending her son to school. "I got a lot of throat clearing." But the law was clear, and it was on her side. She was able to let her son do what she had wanted to do and could not. She didn't use a standard curriculum, but there were books all over the house. "He'd arrive at my bedside with a book and say, 'Let's read, Mom!' We were doing so much stuff I thought, Why make it a lesson thing? It didn't make sense to me," she says.

But unschooling was a choice that few people could understand. She kept in touch with John Holt, and at one point told him, "I don't know anybody who doesn't think I'm nuts." When people contacted him, he started referring them to Plent, and a network soon emerged. About ten people had a meeting, and afterward went back to their own neighborhoods and starting looking for others who had made the same kind of educational choice. There were more than anyone had imagined, and the number kept growing. "I found my phone number got listed so many places that I was on the phone all the time, and getting mail from people in the same shape I'd been in a few years ago. I knew how it felt. Before I knew it we were having meetings all over the place, and I'd be writing ten letters a day," Plent says. "I was bombarded with great people. Every other phone call somebody was doing something amazing." She started an annual conference for New Jersey unschoolers. Hundreds of people came to those conferences, and it was not unusual for those who had felt isolated, eccentric, and decidedly fringe to take comfort in the fact that whatever else they might be, they weren't alone.

What We Learned from Conferences

The conference was an important source of both moral support and nitty-gritty information about how to approach the educational enterprise. At the first conference Martine attended, she participated in a workshop exploring the techniques to deal with the symptoms of ADD. None of our children ever received such a diagnosis but it was often a struggle for some to focus. So Martine listened with interest to such ideas: allowing the child to stand while working, or to use headphones and music to mask ambient noise and minimize distracting conversation, or to make the work surface a relaxing color by using a colored mat under the work. Although an "authority" presented and monitored the workshop, fellow homeschoolers joined in to freely share whatever ideas had worked for them.

At the same conference Manfred Smith, principal director of The Learning Community International, mentioned the physical changes that affect the adolescent brain. Talking with him afterward, Martine realized that issues that she had considered to be matters of discipline could be matters of physical development. Sometimes patient waiting was the best pedagogy. At another conference, a panel titled "Special Circumstances" reinforced that message. A presentation by William Moskowitz, a "behavioral optometrist," emphasized that learning to focus the eyes was a developmental milestone that had to occur before reading skills could develop. In a private conversation after the presentation, Moskowitz confirmed that, in some cases, trying to force reading too soon could bring on symptoms like those of ADD.

This was important because one of our children had not yet begun reading, despite his early interest in words, clear intelligence, the family's culture of reading, and his interest in books. We took the risk—a risk we could not have taken were he in school—and stopped pushing reading exercises for a while. We also stopped practicing writing letters, which had been an immense source of frustration and a disciplinary miasma. Instead of demanding that he write, Martine just gave him crayons to color more or less difficult coloring sheets and watched his progress. It worked out splendidly.

The annual Unschoolers Network conferences were like market fairs, where a lot of villages were represented. Like market fairs, they included opportunities to buy and sell, in this case mostly used books, but more important were the information and encouragement exchanged. Even as the Unschoolers Network grew, Plent insisted on one thing: a loose organization, minimal structure. "I'd get a call from somebody saying, 'I want to form a chapter,' and I'd shudder and say, 'Don't do that, because then we'll need a president, a vice president. Just start a group. I'm just trying to connect people.'

Things rise, they fall, out of somebody's need. Often strong organizational types start them, and sometimes strong organizational capability is what crashes them to the ground. I've told reporters we're cussedly independent people. If you put a hundred homeschoolers in a row and asked them a question, you could get ninety-nine different answers."

As Plent's experience suggests, the word "homeschooling" is a bit misleading. It seems to connote that children spend their days sitting at home with Mom and doing schoolwork in isolation. That's a false impression. Few if any homeschoolers work in isolation. The strength of homeschooling is in the way it frees people to work together—and not just with other homeschoolers.

Expansive Networks

We'd chosen homeschooling in order to be independent, so we looked for opportunities for the children to develop their interests and skills, and joined whatever clubs or groups provided those opportunities. Because homeschooling was so time-efficient, we were able to take advantage of many of these. We deliberately made our network wider than the homeschooling community and got involved in activities that were open to us on the same basis as they were open to schoolchildren.

The social life of homeschooled children can be as broad and diverse as they and their parents choose to make it. They needn't be constrained by the peer group in a particular school, or neighborhood, or church, or even by a particular home-school group. Homeschooling also allows the flexibility to co-operate with people over a much wider geographic area than a typical school district. The radius of our routine home-schooling groups, those in which we participate physically, is about fifty miles. That is to say, most members live within fifty miles of the center, and the center is within fifty miles of our house. But the center changes, depending on the group. We may drive twenty or twenty-five miles north one day, and the same distance south another, to participate in a group with others who have driven a similar or longer distance from any direction.

Of course, online groups make the idea of a center or a radius irrelevant—other members may be anywhere in the world. Because homeschoolers are autonomous, we can take initiative, make decisions quickly, and come together and move apart when and as we choose in response to changing opportunities and needs. Among the reasons we come together is to build networks of personal relationships for mutual sup-port and sharing of information. These relationships are in part responsible for the fact that, as one researcher found, "for many home schooling mother-teachers, home-schooling acts as a stress-reducing educational alternative."[18] Such support networks can also help a mother become a success at home-schooling even though she may have little education herself.

Although homeschool parents are much more likely than the general population to have attended college, almost 12 per-cent of homeschooled students have parents who went no further than high school, according to U.S. Census data.[19] We know several homeschooling mothers with little or no college. In fact, one of the most impressive homeschooling moms of our acquaintance left high school at age sixteen and never went back. Yet she not only homeschooled her own children into top-tier colleges but has also continued tutoring or coaching other homeschooled children to acceptance by the most selective universities.

As our children got older, we found ourselves working more with other homeschoolers. For example, a friend, Martha Nowik, wanted to teach chemistry to her daughters but thought it would be fun to have a bigger group than just her daughters (although she had seven daughters at the time, only two were the right age for chemistry). So we all got together once a week for chemistry class, with Martha handling instruction. Later Martha, whose training is in music, organized a homeschooled choir with dozens of members from throughout central New Jersey. Later still, we organized the Carpe Diem Forensics Association. Nowik children, Millman children, and those from a number of other families have competed at the high school and middle school level in public speaking events alongside students from public and private schools.

Somewhat more formal was a Shakespeare troupe, the Merely Players, founded by Amy Mandelker, an authority on Russian literature. A professor at the City University of New York, Amy earned her fame writing about Tolstoy. But she is also a single mother and a homeschooler who about four years ago, when her son was middle school age, brought some homeschooled children together to read Shakespeare. Originally, she had in mind a reading group, but the children wanted to perform, and one thing led to another. The Merely Players evolved into a serious youth theater troupe, meeting weekly to study and rehearse, staging one new Shakespeare play a year, in the language Shakespeare wrote—no dumbing down here. Amy preps older members to compete in the English-Speaking Union's activities, and generously gives her time to develop musical talents and support her protégés as they win roles in community theater and move on to college. The Merely Players have participated in several Shakespeare festivals, including Princeton Repertory's Shakespeare in the Square, and the joint Folger Library/Drew University project, Shakesperience.

Andrew Schlafly, son of the famous political activist and homeschooler Phyllis Schlafly, conducts formal classes for homeschoolers on such topics as economics, history, composition, and government. The classes draw students from all over the state, and from a range of political, religious, and homeschooling perspectives. Schlafly himself is staunchly conservative, and one of the great virtues of his classes is his openness to debate and discussion with those whose views differ from his own. Although the classes meet in a church hall, they have helped our young sons to get some exposure to a "classroom" environment, to learn to deal, early on, with formal tests, grades, and papers. Students regularly pass CLEP (College Level Examination Program) and other tests to gain college credit for their work.

Small is a virtue in homeschool groups. Smaller groups foster and benefit from personal trust and personal relationships that disappear when groups grow too big. For example, a founder of one of the larger homeschooling groups in northern New Jersey told me that issues of liability were becoming a serious problem as her group grew. Parents who had known and trusted one another when the group was small were beginning to worry about the possibility of lawsuits if an accident happened during a carpooling trip or on a playing field.

Ticking down a list of homeschool groups in which we participate or with which we have contact, three things seem particularly remarkable. One is their ability to tap the skills and expertise of members. The second is their willingness to do so—because groups are small, every member usually has a say. Groups that don't listen and don't value skills tend to wither, because people don't like being part of such groups. The third is the ease with which people move back and forth among groups, bringing information and news. Skilled people willing to share their time and expertise in groups that value them, and able to get the information that they need to invest their social capital effectively, can be powerful indeed.

The Little Way Homeschooling Cooperative, for example, includes homeschooling families from diverse backgrounds, who can choose from a menu of classes in forensics, music, art, and drama, as well as Latin, science, and gym. The weekly classes offer age-appropriate activities for toddlers through high schoolers.

A More Structured Approach

Not every homeschool group adopts the unstructured approach of the Unschoolers Network or the openness of the Little Way Homeschool Cooperative. An example of a much more carefully controlled group is the Friendship Learning Center, an activity of New Jersey's Somerset County Christian Parent Educators Association (SCCPEA), where Pat Fritz has brought corporate management disciplines to the leadership. This center, an enrichment program for children of SCCPEA members, meets twice a month during the ordinary school year. When I spoke with her, Fritz was just about to begin her second year as leader, a job she approached with some impressively sophisticated analytical tools and leadership strategies.

She has a background in education, like Nancy Plent, but she has also worked in the hospital and the pharmaceutical industries. A native of New Jersey, she earned a master's degree in clinical audiology at the University of Tennessee, taught special education in California, returned to New Jersey, and eventually became director of clinical audiology at Robert Wood Johnson Hospital. As she sought advancement opportunities, she eventually found herself working in drug development at Schering-Plough, traveling extensively. In 1990 she married, and her first child was born in 1992. She went back to work after five months of leave but did not want to travel, and "ended up with work that no one else wanted to do."

She left the company to become a full-time mom and be-gan to homeschool when her son was ten years old, putting together his own computers, and bored with school. She didn't jump into homeschooling, though. She even scheduled an appointment with the superintendent, hoping, as she says, to "find some middle ground between public school and homeschooling." The superintendent told her frankly that the school couldn't offer a program that would allow her son to do his best—but he did recommend someone to whom she might talk about homeschooling. (As her experience sug-gests, a homeschooler's relationship with the local school can be quite cordial. People should always begin any interaction with school officials in the expectation that it will not be an-tagonistic.)

Thus, in 2002, she found her way to the Friendship Learning Center. She enrolled her son and daughter and vol-unteered where she could make a contribution. When, in 2005, the woman managing the center stepped down, Pat Fritz agreed to take the helm.

She moved immediately to implement a management sys-tem that would reflect what she'd learned in industry and from reading business and motivational books. Her first step was to put together a leadership team "of strong women who would tell me their opinions." She undertook a formal survey of the center's members to assess both skills and needs, then followed up with a series of focus groups called Dessert with a Purpose. (Each member of the leadership team invited a small group of members home for dessert and coffee and conversation about the center.) The survey found a wealth of skills and capabilities among the center's members. The homeschooling mothers were current or former nurses, schoolteachers, accountants, professional actors and musicians, medical researchers, artists, professionals in business and finance, nutritionists, travel agents, and customs officers. Their husbands included computer professionals, public school teachers and administrators, entrepreneurs, physicians, security officers, engineers, and physicians.

The center was able to draw on this newly discovered pool of skills almost immediately. A dad agreed to teach a computer course. A mother with Broadway acting experience taught a theater workshop. A mother who had taught science at the high school level stepped in to teach a chemistry course. The discovery that several of the fathers were serious woodworking hobbyists with well-equipped shops led to the idea of starting a woodworking group.

The survey and focus group provided data on what people wanted from the center, what they liked, and what they would like to see improved. Pat Fritz worked with her statistician husband to analyze the data using statistical techniques familiar in the consumer goods industry, and prepared two reports: comprehensive results for the leadership team, and summary results in impressive bar chart format for the general membership.

"I want to think big," she says, "about what we want this group to be for our kids."

We are not members of the Friendship Learning Center, although we have occasionally participated in activities on the periphery that are open to nonmembers. I think it is impressive not only as an example of a highly organized homeschooling group but also because it illustrates how homeschooling mothers are bringing to homeschooling the intellectual capital they have developed in corporate management and other organizational environments. It is also noteworthy that Pat's approach is still, for all its rules and analysis, a bottom-up approach. She gauges her success by the response of her market, measured in her surveys of the membership.

When needs change or when opportunities come up, Fritz and her leadership team respond to them. One of the members of the team has been exploring the possibility of expanding beyond an enrichment program to offer for-credit courses at the high school level. No one mandates or directs this from above. The homeschoolers in the Friendship Learning Center do not need clearances, school board approvals, votes on bond issues, or anything else in order to pursue their educational mission. They have made a major change in the way their program works, and they may make another major change in a year or two if new needs require it. The Friendship Learning Center is not exactly typical of homeschooling groups; I am not familiar with another homeschooling organization as self-consciously corporate-managerial in its style. In another sense, though, it is quite typical. Numerous groups in our homeschooling village tap a similar spirit of volunteerism and self-investment, and benefit from the skills of highly educated, experienced women. They just tap it in different ways. That diversity is a strength of homeschooling.

Brokerage and Closure

Homeschooling, as a movement, as a system, is stronger for having a variety of groups within it, and every group by definition needs a certain degree of exclusivity if it is to be a group at all. Without boundaries that include and exclude, a group can have no definition, no identity, and—most crucial—no trust. In his study of social capital, the sociologist Ronald S. Burt of the University of Chicago[20] refers to a balance of "brokerage and closure" in groups. Burt sees organizations and societies as galaxies of groups, separated like stars by empty space. Closure keeps groups from disintegrating; brokerage bridges the empty spaces that separate them, offering groups the challenge and opportunity of new discoveries.

Burt illustrates his analysis with the story of the Civil War's disastrous Battle of Fredericksburg, in which Union troops repeatedly attacked Confederate defenses, and repeatedly failed, at a cost of over twelve thousand casualties. Union field officers recognized that General Ambrose Burnside's strategy of conventional attack was hopeless, but field officers and headquarters officers were two distinct groups separated by a distance both physical and sociological. Closure—the tendency of a group to close ranks against outsiders—would have prevented the generals from accepting what the field officers said even if the field officers had dared to challenge the generals' conventional wisdom. There was no one to broker between the two groups, no one trusted by both the field and the headquarters and able to carry the truth from one to the other.

Closure is necessary because it determines the boundaries of a group, provides a context for trust, and defines its norms, acceptable behaviors, and attitudes. But there can be too much of a good thing. Closure tends to eliminate variety. Groups where closure is too strong cut themselves off from valuable new information and ideas, such as the information that the attack on Confederate defenses could not possibly succeed. Brokerage is the antidote—brokers introduce novelty, diversity, and innovation. Both brokerage and closure are necessary, in due proportion, to build social capital.

The Friendship Learning Center group defines its boundaries by a shared commitment to a certain sort of Christian faith. Yet brokerage also occurs. Pat Fritz's son, for example, was on a robotics team organized by the family of Haya and Darrell Gray, whom we know from the Merely Players—the Shakespeare troupe in Princeton. But the Shakespeare troupe has no particular religious identity—it includes Jews, Messianic Jews, some agnostics, and evangelicals and other Christians, including Catholics. Religious beliefs are no barrier to cooperation among homeschoolers.

Brokers sometimes overlap. Another family from the Shakespeare troupe, that of Mary Alice and Stephan Landau, introduced us to Pat during a Biography Day, which Mary Alice organized. Mary Alice is an active broker and connector, and we have a surprising number of points of contact in common despite differences in our homeschooling approaches.

Within the homeschooling community, there is a lot of

that sort of cross-membership among groups. Homeschool-ers form groups to address needs. One need, for some, may be the company of co-religionists, so there are groups that provide it. But that is only one need, and most homeschool-ers need more than just the company of co-religionists—and so they look to other groups. Like stars in Burt's social galax-ies, homeschool groups form by closure but bridge to one an-other through brokerage. The combination of brokerage and closure makes homeschoolers a very well networked popula-tion. Information moves quickly when it needs to. Home-schoolers and homeschool groups are so diverse that they may really have nothing in common except the fact that they homeschool. But a threat to their independence can bring them out like fire ants.

Such a threat occurred in January 2004. We found our-selves driving to the statehouse in Trenton on the last day of the legislative session. The Delaware River was full of ice, thanks to a record-breaking cold snap. But within the few previous days, our e-mail inboxes had filled with warnings and alerts, some passed on by homeschooling friends, some sent directly from homeschool groups, networks, e-lists, and such of which we were members. Some months earlier there had been yet another scandal in New Jersey's notoriously scandal-prone Department of Youth and Family Services. A child in the custody of the department had been placed in the care of a mother who claimed to be homeschooling him. When he was discovered rummaging through trash for some-thing to eat, a powerful assemblywoman apparently decided that the problem wasn't the child welfare bureaucracy, nor the caseworkers who were responsible for the child. She decided that the problem was homeschooling, and introduced a bill that would tighten regulations on homeschoolers.

The rumor was that she was determined to move it to a vote on this, the last day of the session, without debate, and that she was powerful enough to do it. This legislator had a reputation for being close to the New Jersey Education Association, the teachers' union in New Jersey. The National Education Association has long opposed homeschooling altogether, and the proposed bill would have helped make it a lot harder. The bill would have required homeschoolers to take tests and physical exams that were onerous, expensive, and not even required of schoolchildren. Homeschoolers decided that they had to stop this bill in its tracks.

A task force had come together almost instantaneously. It included representatives of ENOCH (Education Network of Christian Home-Schoolers), New Jersey's umbrella organization for Christian homeschooling groups, and Scott Woodruff, an advocate from the Home School Legal Defense Association (HSLDA), another Christian group. But it also included such prominent unschoolers as Nancy Plent and Tim Haas. It included Catholic homeschoolers. Many of them had not worked together before, even though they had been active in homeschooling in New Jersey for decades. All of them had put the word out to their contacts and networks that homeschoolers had to make themselves seen and heard in Trenton. The urgent twenty-first-century alarm soon found its own way, without centralized direction, via various random, almost untraceable routes to the people who needed to know.

The old state trooper in the parking lot gatehouse gave our boys an avuncular smile and directed us over a meandering route around the full lot to a lawn where, watched by another trooper in a patrol car, the overflow crowd was parking on the frozen grass. We followed a black couple and their three children through the heavy bronze doors of the New Jersey statehouse and signed our names in a book at a security desk. We passed through a metal detector. A younger trooper, less friendly than the one at the gatehouse, gave us blue plastic visitor badges that we clipped to our coats. His partner pointed us toward the stairs. At the top we saw scores of homeschooling parents and children milling around, some clutching big manila envelopes and trying to find their legislative offices, others looking for the visitors' gallery in the Assembly, still others asking one another why the state police were coming through the hallways and pressing people to the walls.

We heard that the state police wanted to eject everyone on the grounds that they were conducting an illegal rally inside the statehouse. But these people weren't shouting slogans or marching or carrying signs or chaining themselves to doors or doing other things symptomatic of a rally. They weren't following a leader or an organizer. They weren't wearing identical hats or T-shirts or other visual clues to suggest united political muscle. In fact, it was hard to see what these families had in common. They had come to Trenton to assert their independence, not to join a group but to defend their right to be left alone. About the only thing they shared was their conviction that they didn't want the state interfering with their children's educations.

When the Assembly convened that day, homeschoolers filled the visitors' gallery. The sergeant-at-arms called for order. The assemblymen and assemblywomen took their seats. Then they stood momentarily while the chaplain led them in a pro forma prayer. Then they sat down again. But by coincidence, perhaps, this happened to be an important anniversary for the NJEA, so the assemblypersons spent some time singing the praises of the teachers and their union. You wouldn't have known just from the speeches that the teachers' union was one of the biggest campaign donors in the state or that it usually got what it wanted because when it went on strike the schools had no choice but to close until the teachers were satisfied. The assemblymen and assemblywomen were too tactful to mention any of that. Instead, they energetically declaimed that the two hundred thousand members of this teachers' union were selfless souls devoted to children, and that whenever the teachers asked for anything from the legislature, it was never for themselves but only and always for the welfare of the children. The orators were delicate enough to avoid mentioning the research that demonstrates teachers unions tend to raise educational costs while reducing educational outcomes.[21]

But the bill did not come to a vote. And several months later, in May, when the same legislator brought it up again, over a thousand homeschoolers came to Trenton again on short notice and heard more than one assemblyperson say that homeschooling isn't broken, and doesn't need fixing.

CHAPTER EIGHT TAKEAWAYS

✓ Homeschooling has been unplanned and uncontrolled. It is a bottom-up enterprise in which individuals make free choices about education. Yet homeschoolers everywhere in the country seem to come together in similar ways. That's the essence of emergence, the creation of similar patterns of order from apparently random events.

✓ It is because homeschoolers are free to come together and separate at will and to try new ways of doing things and new things to do that homeschooling works as well as it does.

✓ We protect our children not from exposure to new ideas but from lack of exposure to new ideas.

✓ Many teachers opt for homeschooling when they are making decisions about how to educate their own children.

✓ Few if any homeschoolers work in isolation. The strength of homeschooling is in the way it frees people to work together—and not just with other homeschoolers.

✓ The combination of brokerage and closure makes homeschoolers a very well networked population. Information moves quickly when it needs to.

NINE

Accepting a College

It's the first day of fall, 2003. I turned sixteen about fifteen minutes ago. I'm surrounded by girls who share a common interest with me. One of them, a petite brunette asks, "How much do you weigh?"

I weigh more than she does.

We sit in a semicircle eyeing each other. I know that any one of them would be delighted to throw her arms around my neck and squeeze until I pass out.

My name is called. I stand and move to the center of a huge square piece of foam ringed with duct tape. I step forward and glance at the referee who motions for us to bow. On his cry, my opponent and I rush toward each other, pause warily, and grip the other's gi jacket. We move about in a strange parody of dance, searching for weaknesses. She moves quickly, and I am hard pressed to find an opening. I sweep, she dodges. She attacks, I move fluidly away, rebalancing myself.

Every match I fight in judo leaves me breathless but full of determination to keep on fighting no matter how big my opponent is. Several years ago I was scared whenever I got on the mat. I began doing judo at the age of seven, and for the first few years I would win or place at most tournaments. Then I hit a plateau. I had seen many people quit judo at this point—the point where they stopped winning, where it stopped being fun. As I faced an opponent and wondered whether she would dive for my legs, or grab for my neck, my entrails would turn to ice.

I had never come across this fear before. My sensei even took me aside and told me that I had to keep on fighting—that the only way that I could get over my fear was by fighting through it. Sensei Yonezuka had told us that he was never studious. He had basically gotten through life on his judo skills until he was retired from competition because he won all the time. Then he opened a dojo and coached Olympic teams. What did he know about fear? But he reached out to explain it in terms of algebra to me, saying, "When you study math, you have to practice and practice. You have to do the problem over and over. Otherwise, you won't be able to solve it."

Not many days later, I was thrown, took a bad fall, and broke my collarbone. I don't handle pain well, and this was excruciating. For a month and a half I sat on the bench and observed classes. During that hiatus I realized that if I let my fear get the better of me I would always be afraid of the next step into the unknown.

After returning to judo I worked hard and began to fight. Although it was not easy overcoming my reluctance to attack, it became clear that I could do what I set out to do. Every time I forced myself to get onto the mat again it became easier to quell the churning of my stomach.

My opponent throws me and we both go down. I flip over so I won't land on my back (which would cause a win), and begin to wrestle her into a pin. I grab her arm and, holding onto the sleeve, place her in a pin. I keep my head low, and begin counting under my breath: one, two, three, four . . . twenty-eight, twenty-nine, thirty. A red beanbag, signifying the end of the match, arches through the air and lands with a thunk a few feet away from my head. I stand up and help my opponent to her feet. We move back to our starting positions, the grand wave of the referee's hand announcing me as winner. My opponent and I bow, shake hands, move back, bow again, and leave the mat. I feel

proud of myself. After reporting my win, I return
to the group of girls and sit again. I run through
some stretches, and watch the next match. Judo
isn't about victory: the struggle is what really
matters.

That was the college admissions essay our daughter Anna submitted with her application package. During her brief stay in the local high school—just one semester—she had gotten to know the guidance counselor. When she showed him her essay he said, "We could never have given you that kind of education here. That shows the importance of your being homeschooled." Anna applied to numerous colleges, some top-tier, some middling. She received acceptance letters and impressive grant offers and financial aid commitments from almost all, and eventually chose Brown.

Our other daughters had similar experiences. The issue for them was not gaining acceptance to a college but deciding which college offer to accept. Scholarships, merit awards, and other forms of financial aid were factors in the decision, of course, but the decision ultimately depended on fit. We had provided our children with a sound start on a liberal education, and had no doubt that they could contribute to the intellectual and social milieu at any college. Through our forensics and other activities, we'd met some of the best students at some of the best schools in the country and recognized that our daughters could hold their own. We approached the college admissions process first as a matter of finding colleges that would provide the community and approach to learning best suited to each child. Then it was a matter of making a compelling case to the admissions office.

We applied to, visited, or corresponded with several dozen colleges considered by our three daughters over a period of five years. Add the college representatives we spoke with at college fairs, and the unsolicited mail that arrived when colleges learned of our daughters' scores on standardized tests, and we've been exposed to several hundred colleges.

The things that are terrific about Amherst are terrific about liberal arts colleges generally. Homeschoolers have obviously had intimacy in teaching and learning, and are likely to duplicate that at Amherst. They're likely to be in classes that average fifteen or less. They will probably develop several mentoring relationships with faculty. I know it's a less affluent group. . . . Twenty percent of this year's (2006) entering class are Pell Grant recipients, and one in five has a family income of less than forty thousand dollars. I don't remember any complaint from the dean's office about academic or social adjustments of homeschoolers.

TOM PARKER, dean of admissions
Amherst[1]

Some schools were so attentive that the deans of admissions sent handwritten notes urging one or another daughter to attend. Some admissions offices demanded voluminous information, then lost the files. Now, one would expect to be courted by lesser schools and ignored by the most prestigious and selective colleges. But the curious thing was that the more selective the school, the more attention the admissions office seemed to pay. We had our best experiences with highly selective schools and our worst experiences with less selective schools.

This led us to wonder again and again, "What are the admissions officers thinking? What are they looking for?" Our first-hand experience with the process, and interviews we conducted for this book, provided some answers to those questions.

The College Admissions Culture

The college admissions profession has a sort of culture of its own. This culture may be more businesslike than many people recognize. In fact, the business side of admissions may sometimes come as a shock to admissions officers themselves.

Says Jim Bock, dean of admissions and financial aid at Swarthmore, "When I was acting dean, one of my first meetings was with the bond raters. I realized that they were gauging the strength of the college based on how many applications we received and how selective we were. When colleges float a bond issue, the interest rate is tied to how selective you are—the more selective, the better investment you are."[2]

John Latting, director of undergraduate admissions at the Homewood campus of Johns Hopkins, says, "There's no question that admissions is one of those areas that gets great scrutiny not only by the bond-rating agencies but also by one's colleagues, faculty, alumni, and others. Admissions is a kind of a signpost, a signal of how the institution is doing. There's a pressure, a need to perform, to produce in a way that can be quantified: number of applications, quality of applications in terms of grades and test scores. But there's another issue too. Incoming students are often one of the most important sources of revenue for the institution. No matter how wealthy, every institution depends on, and bases budgets on, expectations about a tuition revenue stream. There's a lot of pressure to meet those expectations, and that is a very serious pressure, because you're talking about jobs on the line if you don't meet with success. Both of these pressures have increased over the years."[3]

Harold Wingood, associate provost and dean of admissions and financial aid at Clark University, is equally forthright: "Ultimately what we do is a business. We are responsible for bringing in students, generating tuition revenues, and balancing financial aid. To stick to the notion that admission is somehow not a business is a mistake. The reality is that this is the way it has always been. What a school looks for in an applicant will be defined by the priorities the institution sets for itself. What people don't want to think about is that we admit people based on our needs and not on the student's needs. Just because a student has his or her heart set on a place is not going to make a difference. What will make a difference is whether the student's profile and characteristics are consistent with our goals and our priorities."[4]

There is nothing particularly crass, mercenary, or unusual about these three admissions officials or the institu-

Homeschoolers are not excluded in the most selective institutions from the expectation of having a strong foundation academically and tested capability but are also not excluded from our expectation that there will be a reflective excellence in other ways, [such as] play first chair, or be part of a soccer team at a high level. Those characteristics and capabilities are also important for the most selective institutions and we read for those. It's not just tested capability or grade capabilities, but how is this person and how will they play, how will they do in the kind of environment we have.

RICHARD H. SHAW, dean of admissions
Stanford[5]

tions they represent. Financial pressures are facts of life in colleges as they are in any other business. Some schools do cross over to the dark side in their attempt to improve their selectivity ratios and standings in the press rankings of colleges. Among college counselors and admissions officers with whom we spoke, it was an open secret that one major Midwestern university regularly conducted mass mailing campaigns soliciting excessive numbers of applications from highly qualified students. The intention was allegedly not to admit these highly qualified students but rather to reject them. For a university to have a high selectivity ratio, it must reject many more students than it admits. This university's admissions office was playing a numbers game to exploit the rankings mechanism. Although it had succeeded in improving its scores on the more widely followed press rankings, that success came at some cost of reputation in the admissions and college counseling communities. Such practices seem to be rare, but the fact that they occur at all illustrates the importance of business and financial considerations in the admissions office.

The business of admissions works a bit differently in state schools from the way it works in private schools. In state schools, for example, admissions professionals often (but not always) have less flexibility and discretion than their colleagues in private schools.

There are also differences from institution to institution. Although college admissions officers have, collectively, a professional culture, they also operate in institutions that have distinctive cultures and histories of their own. One shorthand definition of such institutional culture, familiar to readers of business books, is "how we do things around here."

Homeschoolers challenge that culture because for most of the twentieth century admitting homeschoolers wasn't something that colleges did. Even now, admitting homeschoolers is something that colleges do rarely, merely because homeschoolers are still a small fraction of the applicant pool. It's important for homeschoolers to recognize these facts, because they directly affect the fate of their college applications. "The excruciatingly competitive colleges that have to turn down eighty to ninety percent of those that apply aren't looking to do favors for kids they don't know," says John Boshoven, past president of the Michigan Association of College Counselors (now called the Michigan Association for College Admission Counseling).[6]

A few admissions officers at public universities have tracked the experience of homeschoolers after admission. Angela Evans, assistant director of admissions at Georgia's

Kennesaw State University, found that freshmen who had been homeschooled "typically performed about three-tenths to five-tenths of a GPA point higher than their peers, generally had a higher SAT score, and earned grades in English and composition higher than their peers."[7] Mike Donahue, admissions director at Indianapolis's IUPUI—a joint-venture urban campus of Indiana University and Purdue—found that the homeschooled "outperformed the regular student population by a significant amount. Their letter grades as a group were almost one letter grade higher than the general population."[8]

More important—and certainly more counter to stereotype—homeschooled students seemed more mature, socially adept, and psychologically well balanced than the general population. Says Evans, "When I have conversations with homeschooled students, they reply with confidence. They're not looking at what I want to hear, they answer honestly. When I talk to high school kids, they're searching for the right answer, with very little introspection. With the homeschooled, there's not that constant need for approval."[9]

At some highly selective schools, homeschooled applicants have made a strong positive impression even without formal tracking studies. Swarthmore's Jim Bock says that the acceptance rate for homeschooled applicants is at least equal to that for conventionally schooled applicants and sometimes higher. "Swarthmore is open to homeschoolers," Bock says. "The Swarthmore pool is selective. We're known among academics but we're not a household name. So when homeschoolers find us they are usually finding us for all the right reasons."[10]

Our homeschooled daughters attend Clark University,

Brown University, and St. John's College (Annapolis), and we have found all three institutions to be very congenial for homeschooled applicants. We were also quite impressed with the University of Chicago. Yet homeschoolers have to be careful about believing reports that this or that institution is "homeschool-friendly." The story of Stanford's brief outreach to homeschooled students is cautionary.

I find that students attracted to Swarthmore are engaged in the life of mind. They like ideas. We don't care if they're well rounded or "pointy." There are students who excel in one thing, and others who excel across board. I've seen that sometimes homeschoolers have a bent—they'll do the math or science, for example, but they really love writing [or vice versa]. . . . They also have had exposure to experiences where you grapple with ideas. It's not just rote memorization. They go to the library on their own, they have life experiences, and that matters, because we have honors programs where you do seminars, and we want people who can speak well and share opinions.

JIM BOCK, dean of admissions and financial aid, Swarthmore[11]

The Short History of Stanford's Homeschool Outreach

In the November/December 2000 issue of *Stanford Magazine*, an enthusiastic article entitled "In a Class by Themselves" spoke of homeschoolers as "a good bet to flourish" and said, "Among the nation's elite universities, Stanford has been one of the most eager to embrace them." During his tenure in Stanford's admission office, director of undergraduate admissions Jon Reider overcame an initial skepticism about homeschoolers and eventually made recruitment of homeschoolers a priority.

"Early on, when we got e-mails and letters from homeschoolers, I wondered, 'Why would you bother? Aren't there good schools near you?'" But then I would meet these kids and I found them interesting," he says.[12] Reider drafted a policy governing admission of homeschooled students, and a six-digit code similar to the code given each high school, so that the admissions office could keep track of its homeschooled applicants and admissions. "It was amazing how primitive our information system was and how simple it was to come up with something," he recalls.[13]

Besides working in admissions, Reider also taught at Stanford. That's an unusual dual role for an admissions professional, and it helped him see the merits of homeschooled applicants from the perspective of the faculty. He felt a special affinity for homeschoolers because of what he calls their "intellectual vitality." Many applicants to elite schools have focused their educational and extracurricular program throughout high school on getting into the "right" college. "It's not about learning, the joy of discovery, the lightbulb going off in your head," says Reider. "That's what homeschoolers understand, and that's what professors understand. So I became their partisan."[14]

Reider conducted an educational campaign on two fronts.

On the one hand, he raised the profile of homeschooling within the Stanford admissions office. Many admissions officers, he says, "come in with the stereotype that homeschoolers have poor social skills, are weird, and won't understand that when the paper's due, it's due, and when the bell rings, class is over. I don't think there's any reason why homeschoolers are any more subject to these forms of deviance than anyone else. It's just that admissions officers don't have the time, and the numbers of homeschoolers are so small, and there's no constituency. There's a constituency for the minority kids, and for the alumni kids, and the math department wants those math kids, but who is fighting for the homeschoolers? It takes someone in the admissions office to say, 'I'll be their advocate.'"[15]

Besides educating the admissions office about homeschoolers, Reider worked to raise the profile of his admissions office among homeschoolers and to help them understand the needs of even well-disposed admissions officers. "Homeschoolers must realize that they have an obligation to provide as much information as possible in as useful a form as possible, not necessarily in boxes but in a way that will help a benevolent reader. Most admissions offices are benevolent. The homeschooler has to appreciate their task," he says.[16]

Reider spoke at homeschooling conferences and wrote for the homeschool press to spread the word that Stanford's admissions office was open to homeschoolers. His campaign was so successful that as a result of Reider's efforts, many homeschoolers still believe that Stanford is particularly friendly to the homeschooled. But Reider left Stanford in 2000 and became director of college counseling at San Francisco University High School. When Reider left Stanford, the outreach to homeschoolers ended.

Richard H. Shaw came to Stanford as dean of admission and financial aid in 2005. "Jon Reider has been gone a long, long time," he said in an interview.[17] Asked about Stanford's outreach to homeschoolers, Shaw answered, "We have no particularly overt or special efforts to attract or engage homeschooled candidates."[18] Asked about the academic qualifications of homeschoolers, Dean Shaw was somewhat ambivalent. "We get homeschooled applicants every year," he said. "We have to work very hard to determine that the work they've done is competitive and to some extent comparable though not the same as that of students that have gone to traditional secondary school and taken traditional coursework at a high rigor level. Many of these kids are highly accelerated, and quite cerebral. The ones we see have high intellectual capabilities. Not all get in, by any means. We really try to see and determine if it's a good fit between Stanford and that student, whether we can meet their needs and also whether they can contribute to our educational environment. We obviously look at academic capabilities. Often homeschoolers test extremely well, and they have pretty good coursework, but we sometimes have to work hard to determine who's teaching them and how they're accruing the coursework."[19]

Dean Shaw also expressed some concerns reminiscent of the stereotypes that Jon Reider fought—stereotypes about the homeschooled students' ability to interact with others and handle the demands of a classroom.

Dean Shaw, for example, described homeschoolers as "isolated": "The one issue for us, and it's important to say, is that when you're a young person in a homeschool environment you're isolated in some ways from the traditional experience of an adolescent, so you may have to work harder outside the classroom. Kids like this might be engaged in academic research, or doing internships, but we also think it's important for them to be involved in things in their community, or in club sports or activities, successful in social environments, socialized as a teenager."[20]

Dean Shaw also expressed some reservations about whether homeschoolers could adapt, "coming from what is nontraditional to what is traditional, to our university, which has a quarter system and courses. For any traditional university environment this is a caveat."[21]

Jon Reider sought homeschoolers out for their "intellectual vitality" when he was at Stanford. At Swarthmore, admissions dean Jim Bock sees homeschoolers "as students who can give back." As encouraging as those attitudes are, it is important for homeschoolers to recognize that such strongly positive impressions of homeschoolers are not the norm among admissions officers. Stanford's story shows that the presence or absence of a single homeschooling champion in the admissions office can make a big difference in the enthusiasm of a university's outreach to homeschooled applicants.

Obstacles to College Admissions and
Financial Aid for Homeschoolers

At some selective colleges and universities, the welcome mat for homeschoolers has been institutionalized. Although admissions officers from elite schools rarely if ever speak or set up recruitment booths at homeschooling conferences, some have recognized that homeschooling is enough unlike conventional schooling to merit special treatment in admissions. Brown's admissions office has taken a rare degree of interest in homeschoolers. In 1999, James Wrenn, professor emeritus of Asian studies at Brown, began an annual review of applications from homeschoolers. He says that the number of applications from homeschoolers has climbed from only seven or eight that year to around eighty in 2007, and his reviews have convinced him that some homeschooled applicants are "pretty spectacular kids."[22]

Elsewhere, though, homeschooled applicants may face an uphill battle. College admissions officers sometimes violate the law by making excessive and unreasonable demands of homeschoolers. As long ago as 1998, the House Committee on Labor and Human Resources referred to such requirements as additional tests demanded only from homeschoolers as "discriminatory."[23] Subsequently, regulations in some states have changed to remove such burdens. Of course applicants to colleges seldom know the vagaries of laws governing admission, and are usually not in a position to contest a rejection letter on grounds of discrimination. As a practical matter, it makes more sense to learn what the requirements are, and deal with them either by complying or by applying to a different school.

Paradoxically, and fortunately, homeschooled students may fare best in the most competitive and selective colleges. In part, this may be because those institutions are accustomed to dealing with students from very diverse backgrounds, including international or alternative schools. In part, it may be because, unlike state schools, they do not have to ration educational access according to standards set by state legislatures and local political agendas. In part, it may be because the more selective schools generally seek the kind of inquiring minds that homeschoolers bring to college. The well-endowed selective schools are also accustomed to encouraging talent with financial aid.

As a general rule, the more open the admissions policy, the less flexibility there is to accommodate the variety of homeschooling experiences. In New York, for many years, homeschooled students could not enroll in state colleges unless they took the GED exam, because they lacked a high school diploma. The regulation has been changed, but the regulation that replaced it still requires that the homeschooled student's curriculum have the approval of the local school district.

The financial aid programs in state schools often seem to penalize the more innovative, creative, and unstructured forms of homeschooling. In Georgia, regulations require that in order to qualify for the HOPE Scholarship, homeschoolers must graduate from an institution accredited by the Accrediting Commission for Independent Study. "I have definitely seen a trend to sacrificing the flexibility and experience that a home education can bring, in order to be compliant with accrediting standards and receive the HOPE Scholarship," says Angela Evans, assistant director of admissions at Georgia's Kennesaw State University. "I've talked with so many families that are willing to forgo breadth of experience and exchange that for a free college education. The bait is simply too tempting."[24] In order to keep bright students in the state, New Jersey state colleges offer free or severely reduced tuition to students who achieve a certain level of scores on the SAT and who graduate at a certain rank in their classes. A homeschooled friend had a strong interest in science and scored a perfect 1600 on the SAT but did not qualify for the scholarship because he did not have class rank. He went to Caltech instead. Another homeschooler in our network, accustomed to winning science fairs and robotics competitions, would not have qualified for the scholarship either, and will be attending MIT. The eligibility rules for that scholarship program made it more rather than less likely that such highly qualified students would leave the state, but it hardly hurt the students themselves.

At some of the most elite schools, homeschoolers may encounter other obstacles. Admissions officers may, for example, be prejudiced against homeschoolers on religious grounds. "The presumption of guilt that you're a Christian fundamentalist is pretty high," says Jon Reider, who fought against that and other prejudices while he was at Stanford.[25] Admissions officers at a sample of America's most selective colleges agreed to be interviewed for this book, and were sometimes quite straightforward about their prejudice. The admissions dean for one prestigious liberal arts college said, "Some homeschool for religious reasons. They do not apply to [name of school withheld by authors], which is very diverse." Sometimes the expression is subtler, as in the case of the admissions dean who suggested that homeschool associations should provide "some sort of description of the diversity of the population. It's not a good thing if admission people buy into a stereotype of one kind or another. Demonstrate that there's a broad variety of motives."

Still common among admissions officers is the suspicion that homeschoolers may be social misfits incapable of getting along with other people and unable to adjust to classmates, roommates, and schedules. No matter how insular, racist, intolerant, or violent a high school may be, no matter how dismally we may remember our own high school careers, no matter Columbine High School, no matter how uncannily realistic movies like *Napoleon Dynamite,* the perception lingers that high schools provide beneficial socialization experiences. An applicant from any high school therefore enjoys, at many colleges, the benefit of the doubt that he is better socialized than a homeschooled applicant. John Latting, director of undergraduate admissions at the Homewood campus of Johns Hopkins, noted, "When you go to a university you have to get by. You have a roommate, professors, et cetera. It's possible that homeschooled students have less experience at that than other students. It's a question about—is there evidence? Can you check the box and say this is not going to be a concern

Every homeschooler is different—they're all different. They come from a variety of educational and family backgrounds and they don't seem to be similar in any particular way. Some are prodigies, some aren't. Some don't have good schools accessible, some have gone to the best schools in America and left. I've seen a broad range, and it's impossible to generalize.

TED O'NEILL, dean of admissions
University of Chicago[27]

for us? So we look for evidence of social activity, participation in things that require interaction with other people, teamwork, learning communities, organizations."[26]

Still, selective private schools may be a better bet for homeschoolers than less selective state schools. At state schools, rules of eligibility for admissions and financial aid are often matters of legislation or regulation. At selective schools, there is more room for an admissions officer to exercise discretion. As Latting's comment suggests, admissions officers at a highly selective school may be looking for evidence that homeschooled applicants don't fit the negative stereotype. Homeschooled applicants who understand what the admissions office is looking for, and who provide it, may be ahead of the game. If nothing else, they'll have the element of surprise on their side.

Dealing with the Admissions Bureaucracy

The details of organization vary from campus to campus, but all college admissions offices do similar things. All college admissions offices receive and read applications, for example, though they may differ in how they read them and what they want to see in them. Since most admissions offices receive thousands and some receive tens of thousands of applications, they have standard rules and policies for handling them. Moreover, like most bureaucracies, college admissions offices tend to prefer easy decisions to hard ones, and like most bureaucrats, college admissions officers dislike risk. Rules help simplify decisions and give at least the appearance of reducing risk. Thus, a college admissions office may require all applicants to submit a high school transcript and a school profile.

Homeschoolers make easy decisions harder, and admissions offices may give conflicting signals about what they want from homeschooled applicants. Although admissions officers commonly express skepticism about grades given to a homeschooled student by a mother, and say that they want more information about the content of the homeschooler's coursework, they often insist on having those grades anyway. This clearly seemed to be the lesson of our experience with transcripts. At first, we checked to see if a narrative transcript would suffice, then provided a detailed description of the work done, the books read, the papers written, and so on, only to get requests from one college after another for a transcript— meaning a standard transcript with a grid of grades and credits. So we rewrote the transcript to put everything in boxes and assigned grades. Interviews for this book confirmed that no matter how rampant grade inflation may be in public schools, there is a prejudice that Mom will be even more lenient (in our case, the reverse is true). But admissions offices demand the box transcript and grades nonetheless. And because they do not trust the grades they have demanded, many schools also demand that homeschoolers submit extra tests—SAT Subject Tests or AP tests—to document that the grade Mom gave them was deserved.

We learned to operate by the rule of thumb that admissions officers view each application from a homeschooler with a degree of suspicion. We prepared our applications as if we were being judged under the Napoleonic Code—that is, presumed to be lying—and felt obliged to provide enough documentation and evidence to convince the judge otherwise. We submitted documentation, and every time a school requested some additional piece of documentation, we included it in the standard package we sent to all schools.

Many homeschoolers seem to do this. "Homeschool applications tend to be thicker files. We get a lot of lists of books," says Swarthmore's Jim Bock.[28] Admissions officers elsewhere also say that homeschooled applicants present thicker application files than students from conventional backgrounds. But they aren't always grateful for the additional material—some complain that they have to work much harder to process homeschooled applications.

Two issues in the review process are especially relevant to homeschoolers:

1. Does the admissions office have a liaison for homeschooled applicants?
2. Does anyone in the admissions office teach?

The second question matters because admissions officers who teach may have had firsthand experience with homeschooled students in the classroom. That kind of experience benefits homeschooled applicants in general, because it helps to demolish negative stereotypes. Ted O'Neill, dean of admissions at the University of Chicago, says, "I teach a class and had two homeschoolers in one class. They were very different. One was a prodigy in physics, the other came from a rural family with many kids schooled at home. One went on to the graduate program in physics, and the other got a master's within the first four years. They behaved differently in class, but I'm not sure anyone would have noticed that one had not been in class since elementary school and the other had been in and out of school. They integrated into the community, were active widely, participated in class."[29]

Admissions officers who teach, and admissions officers who told us that they consider themselves to be working for the faculty, generally had positive things to say about homeschooling and homeschoolers. This doesn't mean that homeschoolers are shoo-ins for admission, but it does mean that they do not have to carry the heavy handicap of a bureaucrat's prejudices through the admissions process.

The first question—Is there a liaison?—matters because applications to selective schools usually meet several stages of review. At many colleges, the initial review is geographic, and one admissions officer reads all applications from a particular geographic region. Geography may be defined at the county level for applicants to an in-state school, or at the state level, or at the regional level. This approach allows an admissions officer to develop familiarity with the schools, rules, and student populations of a particular region. But homeschooled students may have little in common with conventionally schooled students in their geographic region. Some colleges merely lump homeschooled applicants with other "nontraditional" applicants, such as applicants who have GEDs instead of high school diplomas. At such schools, the admissions officers reviewing homeschooled applications are unlikely to be very knowledgeable about homeschooling.

Other colleges, however, make a special effort to identify homeschooled applications and assign specialists to review them. At Clark University, Harold Wingood explains, "We consider homeschooling as if it were a geographic territory. It's handled by our director of admissions and my associate dean because she has the most experience. Very often homeschooled kids require some additional attention or need additional information."[30]

At the University of Chicago, homeschooled applications go directly to the attention of Dean of Admissions Ted O'Neill, who sometimes conducts the admission interview himself. "We do get interviews on occasion, though they aren't required, and we do sometimes get testimony from a lot of people, sometimes more than the three letters required. Special talents are usually abundant in these students—music or debate or sports," he says. Yet the homeschooled student may need to supply more documentation than the conventionally schooled in order to convince O'Neill and his colleagues that admission is warranted. "Frequently the writing carries quite a bit of the weight of the application," O'Neill says. "Sometimes we get more than enough—college grades, grades from tutors, reports from teachers of all kinds, sometimes test scores, sometimes AP grades, sometimes SAT Subject Tests. We'll probably pay more attention to things like that for a homeschooler, and we hate to say that because we normally don't, but in the case of homeschoolers we probably do."[31]

At Johns Hopkins University, the review process moves in layers. The first layer is a geographic review, and the second layer is a review based on academic interest or concentration. In the third and final layer, all applications from the homeschooled go to Undergraduate Admissions Director John Latting, who explains that "we need to get these folks together and look at them in the same way at some point in the process."[32]

At Swarthmore, similarly, the first review is geographic, and regional specialists read all applications from their regions, including those of homeschoolers. Then, the homeschooled applications go either to Dean of Admissions Jim Bock or to another staff member familiar with homeschooling. "I don't want some rookie to hurt that applicant by misinformation," Bock says. "We don't want them lost in the shuffle, and you can't compare them to private or public school students. You have to know they're all different." For example, a parent usually writes the counselor recommendation for a homeschooled applicant. "We don't usually encourage parent recommendations, but we do from homeschoolers because that's who the adviser was," says Bock.[33]

Our College Choice

After more than a decade of homeschooling, we saw college as an opportunity for our children to experience an academic community that would extend and deepen the liberal education that we had begun. Living on campus would be important, but it would have to be the right campus, one where our daughters could participate fully both in extracurricular opportunities and in classes.

We also looked at college as an investment—not only of money but of time as well. The most important college cost is the opportunity cost. By attending one college, you accept a set of opportunities, and the cost of those opportunities is the opportunities you forgo at some other college. In fact, sometimes the opportunities you forgo extend beyond college, as when students incur massive debts and thereby limit their opportunities to explore and experiment after graduation. They pay a price in freedom for the debt they have incurred, because they have to find work almost immediately and begin to pay the debts.

Just as we had asked ourselves what the purpose of education was when we began homeschooling, we carefully considered the purpose of college as we planned the investment of time and money. For homeschoolers, acceptance into a good college is wonderful validation of our efforts. Yet college assures neither happiness nor success. Those who lack a college degree may overestimate its value, just as those who have it often seem to underestimate its worth. The lack of a college degree seems to haunt people, to undermine their confidence, and may indeed close some doors for them. Research demonstrates that those who graduate from four-year colleges make more money, have more confidence in their judgment, are less authoritarian, enjoy a wider range of social and cultural opportunities, and even have healthier children than the less well educated.[34]

Yet one may question whether these advantages are a matter of causality or mere correlation. Is it that college gives people these personal characteristics, or that these personal characteristics lead people to find their way to college? It may be that those with the character, intelligence, will, and perseverance necessary to graduate from a four-year college might have done as well without the degree, just as homeschoolers have done very well even without high school diplomas.

After our years of homeschooling, we know that there is little that we cannot learn on our own. For us, then, undertaking college must not be just about further learning but about something else too—personal growth and development, certification, networking, validation, acquiring specialized knowledge, laying down the credentials to forge a career, and so forth. College is an investment, first, of time. In most cases, a student will spend at least four years at it. Although community college courses and AP credits can sometimes transfer and can sometimes reduce the time one might need to spend accumulating credits, our aim wasn't to minimize the time spent studying toward a degree. We thought in terms not of attending a college but of becoming part of a college. So we paid particularly close attention to what our daughters might become part of.

Information Resources and Selection Criteria

One source of information was debate tournaments. Several colleges in our region host debate tournaments for high school debaters, and we had visited campuses to compete in these tournaments. Because college students usually run the tournaments, we found that we could get a fairly accurate impression of the character of student life just by what we saw of these students. Our daughters refused to consider two of the Ivy League schools because they found the students in charge of the debate tournaments to be inept, indifferent, arrogant, or unwelcoming. We also paid close attention to the workers at the bottom of a college's status ladder. We made it a point to visit as many schools on our list as possible, and we made it a point to eat in the school cafeteria, where we looked at the students and also at the help. We particularly remember one liberal arts school, ranked among the top twenty in the *U.S. News & World Report* list, for the beaten-dog manner of its cafeteria workers. The students did not acknowledge or talk to them at all—indeed, did not even seem to notice them. The workers were taciturn, did not meet our eyes, seemed unhealthy and unhappy, and did not talk even when they sat at the same table to eat lunch together after most of the students had left. We also remember another school, ranked somewhat lower in the lists, where the woman swiping cards in the cafeteria had the manner of a grandmother welcoming the students into her kitchen. She knew our student hosts and had a long conversation with them both as we came in and as we departed.

We wouldn't use a cafeteria experience as the main criterion for a college decision, of course, but such details contribute to a big picture. The admissions officers themselves can be a good indicator of a college's real character, not necessarily for what they say but for how they say it. At the school with the grandmotherly cafeteria worker, Martine sat for a while waiting while one of our daughters was being interviewed for a scholarship. She noted that the receptionist in the admissions office was warm and friendly, and that the student guides dropped by sometimes, even when they didn't have a tour, just to say hello. At the school with the sullen and taciturn cafeteria workers, on the other hand, the admissions office receptionist seemed remote and impersonal, and shortly after a conversation gave no indication of recognition or acknowledgment when we encountered her outside the office. At another school that was making an aggressive outreach to attract students who had done well in the PSATs, the admissions officers did not seem capable of putting together an English sentence without making several errors of grammar and syntax. We encountered more than one school, even some highly selective ones, where admissions representatives were less polished or less well informed than one might expect, whether the office's primary motivation was business, service, or promoting the institution's image.

We visited campuses while classes were in session and tried to form an impression of the student body. One Midwestern school, disproportionately populated with students wearing black clothes, butch cuts, cellophane hair color, and piercings, seemed to have assembled an entire student body by selecting the two or three brightest nonconformists from each high school up and down the East Coast. The problem was that these students had clearly modeled themselves as nonconformists in high school, and they had all nonconformed in the same way. So here they all looked like conformists.

Treatment of homeschooled applications was an important consideration, of course. We have gone through the college application process three times, and it always seems that after years of stretching outside the box, this process required us to contract and try to fit into a box in order to present ourselves. Despite numerous studies indicating that homeschoolers outperform the conventionally schooled, suspicion and prejudice linger in college admission offices. Admissions officers by and large expect homeschooled applicants to provide more documentation, more test scores, more references, more writing samples, more lab reports, and more proof of their achievement than students applying from conventional school backgrounds. *The Journal of College Admission* noted "unnecessary barriers" to admission of homeschoolers and wrote, "If schools do not require certain admission criteria of other applicants, they must reassess the fairness of a policy required *only* of homeschool applicants."[35] Admissions officers interviewed for this book acknowledged that they often look for more documentation from homeschooled applicants than from other applicants.

Happily, we had been collecting credentials for years. In

spring of 2002 Bridget had taken a trial SAT. We took the PSAT quite seriously, and the SAT. Debate, judo, fife-and-drum, part-time jobs, volunteering, and community college courses provided ample documentation of socialization and academic achievement. Martine had first structured a narrative transcript when the girls applied to take classes at the local community college several years earlier. This narrative portfolio became the foundation for the college application package, though considerably refined.

People often choose homeschooling because institutions matter and there's a decision that schooling at home will be better than membership in public school or private schools that are available. But that's as close to a common denominator as you can get. . . . People should be very comfortable with the decisions they've made and want to explain them or give the logic, the history behind it. Whenever you know more about something, it's easier to go ahead and make an offer of admission. So they should address "Why homeschooling?" It's in their interest to do that, to give a complete and confident accounting of the important educational decision they've made.

JOHN LATTING, director of undergraduate admissions Johns Hopkins[36]

One common thread, of course, was financial constraint, but the financial constraint proved to be less binding than many guides and news articles had led us to believe. Living on one income in New Jersey, where we paid some of the highest property tax and insurance costs in the nation, we were very much aware of the cost of college and the inadequacy of our own savings to cover it. So we tried to include on our list some schools where tuition and other costs were extremely low. But we also looked for schools that "meet need"

Screens

We developed several screens to evaluate colleges. Those schools that passed through the most screens became our focus.

Screening Criteria (in alphabetic order)

- Academic concentrations available
- Ambience (campus life, dorms, cafeteria, social life, alcohol and drug issues, etc.)
- Bookstore (did it stock an eclectic mix of books, or the bare minimum needed for coursework?)
- Campus culture (including quality of staff and treatment of blue-collar employees)
- Dormitory life
- Extracurricular life (sports, clubs, churches, volunteerism, etc.)
- Finances and financial aid
- Homeschool admissions policies
- Library quality, hours, facilities
- Networking opportunities and alumni outreach
- Proximity/ease of travel
- Town-gown relations (we checked community and campus newspapers, and talked to cabbies, police, and even hotel staff about the local college)

or come close, and especially favored those that also offer merit scholarships. All the Ivies and many other highly ranked colleges and universities state that they meet need. Numerous others also offer substantial merit scholarships, and often supplement them with need-based aid.

Incidentally, while each college gives a straightforward representation of tuition costs and room and board, it is important to look beyond these costs to hidden costs. The biggest surprise for us has been the variation in health insurance charges. Students who are not covered by other insurance often must enroll in the university's medical plan. We've found that medical insurance can range from as low as a few hundred to as high as a few thousand dollars a year. It is possible to waive this coverage, but the waiver paperwork is due well before the annual tuition bill arrives. Two more hidden costs are travel and books. Some colleges consider a hundred dollars to be an adequate annual travel allowance, no matter how far away the student's residence is, but this would hardly cover travel to and from the school for breaks. The cost of books is one of the least predictable but often most easily managed of expenses. By planning ahead and tapping the online used-book markets, we've saved hundreds of dollars.

The Colleges We Joined

Bridget, our first daughter, wound up choosing a school that we had never heard of before it contacted us. Because we had anticipated including AP test scores in our application

We want to know not only about academic achievement and interest but about what else they're interested in that might set them apart from other bright tigers.

We ordinarily interview people who apply. That can be particularly helpful for people who are homeschooled. It can be helpful in helping us understand what the homeschool experience has meant. The fundamental question we ask every time is: what has the applicant done with what he had, whatever set of opportunities and limitations that might be. Homeschooling is another set of opportunities.

MARLYN MCGRATH-LEWIS, *director of admissions, Harvard*[37]

package in order to document our work as homeschoolers, she had taken the tests earlier than many public school students do, in her junior instead of her senior year. Among the tests she took was the AP Human Geography test, and she subsequently received several mailings from Clark University about geography, the international studies stream, and other subjects of interest to her. Each of the girls received boxes full of mail after their PSATs, because colleges target mailings to students who do well on those tests. The AP subject tests can also draw mail, especially if the school has a priority of attracting students to study particular disciplines. We tried to open and skim material from each new college. Clark's several mailings were interesting, informative, and enticing, and included information on special scholarships for which Bridget qualified and the incentive of a voucher for a free application filing. So we added Clark to the list, in part because it was easy to do so. Clark was a Common App school—that is, it used the Common Application—but it did ask for supplements and essays. Bridget, thanks to her experience in debate, had developed a knack for writing good essays under time pressure.

After spending Presidents' Day weekend at a debate tournament at Harvard, Martine and Bridget took advantage of being in Massachusetts to visit both Wellesley and Clark. First impressions were not exhilarating. They rode a bus from Boston to Worcester, a depressed, formerly industrial town that is home to five colleges and universities. Clark's location on the dismal area of Main South was dispiriting, but Clark's student body seemed engaged and alive, even in midwinter. Students staffed the admissions office and they were enthusiastic. Having visited several colleges where even the admissions office was depressing, we found that quite impressive. If even the people marketing the school can't show some school spirit, what can one expect elsewhere on campus?

We happened to know some people who had lived in Worcester, and we discovered that an old friend and colleague was now teaching at Clark. We learned that at Clark, there's no town/gown friction. Clark gives back to the community and offers several local scholarships as well. One general scholarship very generously rewards applicants based on volunteering. Moreover, people who know Clark rank it very highly academically, and it has recently received favorable attention from guidebooks and rankings: Loren Pope's *Colleges That Change Lives*, Jay Matthews's *Harvard Schmarvard: Getting Beyond the Ivy League to the College That Is Best for You*, and others. Clark's motto impressed us: "Challenging Convention, Changing Our World." So did the dining room chairs

Some of the very best students that come to Clark have been homeschooled. I can think of several of them who have come through here and made a huge difference. The one thing I always worried about was their socialization and whether they were going to be able to fit into this environment, and that's not been an issue at all.

HAROLD WINGOOD, associate provost,
dean of admissions and financial aid
Clark University[38]

embossed with the motto *Fiat lux*. Clark more than met our screens, and the experience has worked out well.

But when our second daughter began the college selection process a year later, we tried to be better organized and more scientific. We set up graphs and ranking systems to try to measure all aspects of each college that accepted her and also to evaluate the financial aid packages. The University of Chicago began as Anna's first choice. After the PSATs, they deluged her with witty postcards encouraging her to link her future to theirs. Since we happened to be traveling through Chicago, we arranged to make a campus visit, and came away greatly impressed by everything the school had to offer. Curiously, though, once she expressed interest, communication stopped and her application for early action was deferred. It felt like a vexing plot twist in a Jane Austen novel.

The University of Chicago did eventually admit her, and did offer a generous financial package. But so did many other schools to which she applied. A visit to Brown convinced her that Brown was where she belonged. Brown is especially relevant because this school showed a rare degree of understanding and appreciation of homeschooling. Everything she encountered there seemed to point to self-determination. For example, while some schools were as disciplined as clockwork in their organization of events for admitted students, at Brown the admitted students received lists of options, meal passes, maps and room assignments at the gate, and an invitation to explore the campus on their own if they pleased. Moreover, students, not admissions staff, ran Brown's admitted-students' day. Brown's academics are outstanding, and the university gives students autonomy to construct their own curriculum, trusting them to assemble a balanced program.

Our third daughter chose a school whose curriculum is quite strict but also in its own way is a perfect fit for a homeschooler. Lena's interests are eclectic and wide-ranging. Art and microbiology have ranked among her passions. But so have music, classics, botany, Chinese studies, and more. She loves learning for its own sake. A friend had recommended St. John's College to us, and the more we investigated, the more she liked it. A visit to the Annapolis campus brought an epiphany— the discovery of a community of people who loved learning for its own sake. Such communities are rare in a system of higher education, whose function is often more vocational than academic. One college guide describes the experience of students visiting this campus and recognizing that they have been "Johnnies" all their lives. While we are not sure that Lena would ever subsume her identity into a group's to this degree, we believe that she can validate the sentiment. St. John's, by the way, no longer submits information to the *U.S. News & World Report* survey. Precisely because that survey is so influential, so high-stakes, and so powerful that it has determined the admissions policies of some marketing-intensive schools, St. Johns's refusal to play the game impressed us favorably.

Fear, Marketing, and Fact

We first considered college in the 1980s. That was the era of the baby boomlet. We saw our first articles about saving for college shortly after we had our first baby. It was scary, and the scare stories continued for two decades, following the baby boomlet through the stages of childhood, adolescence, and young adulthood. What was it that signaled publishers to stoke anxiety with articles and books about getting into, affording, or staying in college? Fear seems to be part of the marketing process—it helps build a sense of urgency to buy and read one particular magazine or book. We read many such books and articles. But we gave ourselves time to calm down well before the actual application process. More important, we were highly selective about which of those books and articles we passed along to the children, and when.

For example, books about college admissions essays can be daunting. We feel that handing one of these books to a second-semester high school junior or senior is a sure recipe for feelings of inadequacy or writer's block. Reading them can be helpful in the eighth or ninth grade, though, when high stakes are not yet imminent, and they can help both students and parent to focus and plan ahead.

There are several things that worked for us, or that we wish we had known, or think everyone should, and we have listed these below. We hope this advice empowers rather than stresses. We have tried to only include information that is particularly relevant to the homeschooled, or that is not commonly available in books on "getting in."

1. **Most high schools start serious planning for college at the beginning of junior year.** Don't wait that long, because as a homeschooler you will have somewhat more to prove than typical students do. Begin by sophomore year, and preferably by eighth grade.

2. **Homeschoolers actually have an advantage, because they know that they don't have a guidance office to rely on.** Many school parents realize too late that guidance offices are understaffed.

3. **Make friends with local school officials and secretaries; do not anticipate hostility.** If your student will be sitting for PSATs or AP tests, you will have to register at the local high school, and this is probably the most convenient location for SAT and ACT tests. The guidance office is also the best resource for local scholarships. If you have a good relationship, they may go beyond providing forms to making a recommendation.

4. **Don't be afraid to contact your local high school guidance office for information (even though they are understaffed).** Many public schools are

already used to providing some services for students of private schools and will expect to extend their help to homeschoolers as well. Do try to contact them when they are not super busy; check the local schedule for regular school deadlines (e.g., drop/add), and be aware that weeks preceding college application deadlines are particularly busy. April and August (before classes begin) are often good times to get acquainted.

5. **The PSAT/NMSQT (National Merit Scholarship Qualifying Test), administered annually in October, functions at least as much as a screen for scholarships as it does as practice for the SAT.** Take the PSAT at least by sophomore year to prepare for the one that counts (junior/third year) if you might rate in the top 2 percent. You can get a rough idea from taking a practice PSAT in a current test prep book. The top 4 percent nationally attains National Merit Commended Scholar status, while the top 2 percent in your state gains National Merit Semifinalist status, and usually, after more paperwork, National Merit Finalist status. Even though the scholarship money is relatively small, the prestige can open doors.

6. **Even if a college says that it does not require SATs or ACTs, it probably will want to see these for homeschoolers.** The ACT, which has always been popular in the Midwest, became much more widely used as the SAT was revised in 2005. The

ACT provides more options and more control over the test results. Some colleges do not ask for additional SAT Subject Tests if you have an ACT. However, if you are in competition for advanced standing through the National Merit Scholarship Qualifying Test (the PSAT), you must provide a substantiating SAT score to advance from semifinalist to finalist status.

7. **Do not wait until senior year for AP tests. Take them as early as possible if you think you can get a good score.** (Sample tests are available online and books that include sample tests are available for review.) That way AP scores can serve as prestigious validators of academic success. Contact the local high school in February; register in February/March. The test is administered in May.

8. **Do not put "AP" next to a course on the transcript if you have not taken the test and included the score on your transcript.** Not all colleges award credit for AP tests; credit depends on the test, rank, and college. CLEP tests, which are widely available, can also gain advanced standing in some colleges, but they don't carry the same prestige that AP tests do.

9. **Some AP courses are offered through distance programs.** For instance, Stanford offers several courses. You need not undertake a specific AP course to sit for a test; self-study can lead to mastery of the material. There are several scholar

awards recognizing students who score well on a minimum number of AP tests.

10. Community colleges vary widely in their quality of coursework (even among departments in the same college), their welcome to homeschoolers, and the availability of courses for high school students. These credits mean the most to four-year colleges in the same state that have articulation agreements and are more familiar with the particular community college. Whether a college recognizes the transfer credit or not, community college courses still play a useful part in a homeschooler's college prep experience, providing science labs, classroom situations, and possible references.

11. Always prepare a narrative transcript and portfolio of work, but also expect to submit a standard grid with boxed-in grades and points and units earned. Templates and suggestions are available online. Those enrolled in a distance school can expect that institution to issue a transcript. Also, some schools will evaluate previous work and issue a transcript with ungraded units of credit for students; more colleges are accepting these as they entertain more questions about grades awarded at regular schools.

12. Many homeschoolers have gained entry to colleges with self-issued transcripts. In our experience, a college's willingness to accept these seemed

to be proportional to the homeschooling policies in its home state. The more stringent the policies, the less flexible toward homeschoolers' applications the college would be. Some families turn to umbrella schools or distance-education programs to have an official transcript and a diploma. Having this documentation helped gain entry to some colleges.

13. If you hope to participate in athletics at a Division I or II school, consult the NCAA Clearinghouse website early to begin preparing the substantiating paperwork that they require from homeschoolers. An official transcript can help in this case.

14. Some sources suggest that time spent in a part-time job will be considered equally with volunteering and other extracurricular activities. We have not found that to be the case. An exception would be a job in which the student starts a business or otherwise exhibits leadership, initiative, drive, or creativity.

15. The first essay that a homeschooled college applicant needs to prepare is a one-page explanation of the reasons for choosing homeschooling and the benefits derived from this experience.

16. Most high schools have internal deadlines weeks in advance of the particular college deadline. This is a very good idea, especially since you will be pulling all the components of your application to-

gether and mailing it yourself. Finishing applications ahead of time provides more time to apply for scholarships.

17. **Always ask at least one more person to provide a reference than an application stipulates.** Since these are not passing through a high school guidance office, there is no intermediary to follow up. That way, if someone gets the flu or is forgetful, you have insurance.

18. **As admissions officers have gained more experience with homeschoolers, their expectations have risen.** Homeschooled students who apply to the more prestigious institutions will be under pressure to show that they have made the most of the freedom and opportunities they have enjoyed.

CHAPTER NINE TAKEAWAYS

✓ We looked at college as an investment—not only of money but of time as well.

✓ After our years of homeschooling, we know that there is little that we cannot learn on our own. A college degree functions as a formal attestation of that learning.

✓ The financial constraint proved to be less binding than many guides and news articles had led us to believe.

✓ Rules help college admissions officers make easy decisions. For example, they may require all applicants to submit a high school transcript and a school profile.

✓ Homeschoolers make easy decisions harder. They don't have standard documentation.

✓ Many schools demand that homeschoolers submit extra tests—SAT Subject Tests or AP tests.

✓ It is something of a victory for homeschoolers to achieve the status of being an inconvenience to admissions officers. Until recently, many schools rejected them out of hand.

- - - - - - -

TEN

Conclusion

Before undertaking this book, we were too busy meeting the demands of every present moment to wonder how all the moments fit together. Now, at our halfway point as homeschoolers, with three children launched into college and three still in elementary and high school, we've paused to consider where we've been.

We have chosen to be free and to educate our children in freedom. In this Land of Liberty, few make that choice. Jack Kerouac wrote in "The Vanishing American Hobo," "There is nothing nobler than putting up with a few inconveniences like snakes and bugs for the sake of absolute freedom." But Jack Kerouac was an eccentric, as were Walt Whitman and Henry David Thoreau and Thomas Jefferson and every prophet sacred or profane stretching back at least to the fugitive who saw a burning bush and came reluctantly back to preach freedom. Those who choose freedom almost always seem to be eccentric misfits, and those who choose slavery almost always seem well adjusted by comparison. Our freedom is always at risk, but we are its only real threat. The smoke of idols, the clang of cymbals, the shouts of apostates din the creed that freedom is too risky, too uncomfortable, too painful to bear. We've seen people start for freedom and then pause to consider how unreasonable a choice it was in light of what everyone around them knew to be true. Many have choked off their lives by limiting their choices to what they could see.

For example, when we married many assumed that in order to live with dignity one had to achieve a certain annual income and a certain stability of career before having children. The perverse message was that the young should not live, should not give life, should not take risks. We know plenty of people who took this message to heart and waited until they had the income and the cars, the house and the second house, the savings and the career post before having children. Many of them waited too long. We took a different view and made a different choice. We found that conventional wisdom was false. Many things that people say are impossible are in fact very possible if you simply live in the present moment, deal with the challenges of that moment, and let the future wait until it becomes present. We found that these two ways of living form two different habits of thought and life. The practice of taking conventional wisdom to heart and always preparing for the future often means that you never really live in the present, and therefore that you never really live at all, because life is only in the present. The future, with its fears and opportunities, is always a figment of our imaginations. The practice of living in the present moment anchors us in reality and truth, and there is enormous power in reality and truth. Anything is possible then.

We were not immune to the fears and anxieties of a society that seems increasingly to be a society of fear, that thrives on fear and induces fear. Newspapers and television news stations thrive on fear and disaster, and financial counselors and politicians seem to prosper best by stirring up fear and then offering a palliative. We were fortunate in that we had good counselors to help us, one or two priests who advised, the example of many saints and sages to guide us to trust God and live, so with their encouragement we did. We accepted our children as they came, and looking back it seems that each one arrived just when another seemed impossible. With one pregnancy came news of a merger that claimed a job, with another the discovery that a company was about to fall apart, with another the simultaneous disappearance of several companies that had seemed to provide a well-diversified and therefore stable financial foundation. All we did was persevere despite our anxieties and our worries.

If courage means to go without fear, we were cowards, because fear has always been with us. The road has been blind and dark. We've never really known what we were doing, where it was leading, how it would turn out. It has been scary. It has been risky. We have just kept going anyway.

That's how we did it and that's how anyone can do it. For those readers who may have read this book wondering how to homeschool, we have to say that the answer is: by persevering. There are many methods and texts and curricula, many organizations and approaches and styles, but we think that no methodology or recipe or formula will give you what you really need. The choice to work together with your children to help them learn is one that you need to make for a reason great enough to sustain you even through doubt and fear. In our case this was simple. There simply was no decent school available to us, none that would offer our children the kind of education we wanted them to have—namely, an education in becoming a free, reasoning, truth-seeking human being. We thought at first that this was because schools in our area were simply substandard. Only later did we learn, as we explained earlier in this book, that schools do not generally consider this to be their purpose at all. Moreover, schools probably could not do this if they tried, because they are institutions and no institution can offer the one indispensable element of this education: a gift of self.

We found in the course of our homeschooling that the most important part of education is a close personal relationship that folds a child in arms of love and deep respect. This is a relationship in which the parent makes a perpetual self-gift. It means that the parent never has a moment for herself (or himself), never ever tries to take anything just for "me." This idea now seems as countercultural as our attachment to freedom. America is all about the self: self-esteem, self-sufficiency, self-improvement, self-service, self-development, self-satisfaction.

It seems to be as much about the self as it is about fear and anxiety, and the more time we have spent trying to make a gift of ourselves to our children, the clearer it seems that there is a connection between attachment to selfishness and fear.

It seems that self is something like the dragon in those pictures of Saint George—it is something hungry and dangerous and you must kill it. You kill it every moment by small choices, little cuts from the sword of love. T. S. Eliot wrote in "Tradition and the Individual Talent" of the artist's continual self-sacrifice, the artist's choice to annihilate his own personality in the effort to obtain something more valuable. To be a homeschooling parent is to make a similar choice. A child, though, is not a work of art. A child is far more than that, so much more that there simply is no scale of comparison. I once spoke with a poet who told me that his poems were like his children, because he worked as long and as diligently creating them and cared as much for them as any parents could work or care for their children. But the poet had no children, and therefore couldn't possibly understand what parenthood means. He could erase from a poem any line he pleased, or write any line he pleased. A parent cannot erase anything from a child, or inscribe anything in a child. A child lives and chooses, has free will, and can love. No poem can.

Parents can make it easier or harder for a child to live and choose and love. Many of our social institutions, and especially schools, make it harder to live and choose and love in freedom. We homeschool so that our children will be able to live and choose and love, to seek the truth in freedom.

• • •

What final principles can we offer as takeaways? What do you need to homeschool? How can you do it? We can offer three:

1. Believe: You can do it. You couldn't do it alone but you won't have to. You should expect to exert all your strength, but if you do you will find others who can offer you a hand now and then when you need it. Homeschooling is an intensively social system. Networks are well developed, homeschooling organizations exist in every state, and resources are plentiful. Believe, but don't believe only in yourself. There is no tradition of wisdom that regards the self as trustworthy or benevolent, so beware of faith in yourself. Have faith that if you give your children what you have, in love, they will prosper. Have faith in them. If you are fortunate enough to believe in God, have faith in God and pray. If you do not believe in God, then believe in truth, because truth is just God's alias, and, like God, truth comes to those who seek it in good faith.

2. Trust: Messages of fear and uncertainty will come from inside and from outside to discourage you and recommend that you give up. Trust that no matter how implausible your formal credentials, no matter how little money you have, no matter how limited your own education may be, you can do this. If you

persevere you will succeed—provided, of course, that you choose the right metrics to measure success. If you choose as your criterion of success the development of your children as free and reasoning human beings with a devotion to the truth, and you persevere in putting their interests before your own, you will succeed.

3. Love: Saint Josemaría Escrivá said, "Love is deeds, not sweet words." When we say "love," we do not mean tender feelings and we do not mean "tough love." We mean self-sacrifice and self-gift. This love that can only come from faith and trust. Give yourself. Sometimes giving yourself means being tender and sometimes it means exercising discipline to help a child grow in strength and character. Always examine yourself to be sure that the choice you are making is not for yourself but for your child, so that your child will grow in freedom and truth. The self is subtle—selfish motives sometimes conceal themselves in the most benevolent-seeming gestures—so conduct the self-examination regularly and diligently.

Those three are the most fundamental principles. The rest will follow from them. You will have to make choices for the opportunities available to you. We happen to live in central New Jersey, a metropolitan region rich in educational institutions, cultural activities, and so forth. But every part of the country—indeed, every part of the world—has opportunities, and the greatest part of homeschooling is helping your child look around and see them and make choices from them. A parent can do this in a way that no institution can. Only a person can give himself to a person, and what a child needs more than anything else is a person to make that gift. Seeing you make that gift is how the child will learn to make it.

We hope that some of what we have written in this book will be useful to you, dear reader. Thank you.

Acknowledgments

Homeschoolers exercise the traditional American virtues of the Amish barn raising or the pioneer settlement. They cooperate in self-reliance. Many friends and acquaintances contributed to our homeschooling experience and, directly or indirectly, to this book. We would like to acknowledge each of them individually, but merely to list their names and tell how and why they have helped would take a book in itself. So we begin by acknowledging the indispensable help of the anonymous. Their anonymity is no reflection on the importance of their contribution. The history of music, literature, and art shows that "Anonymous" has done more to shape culture than any named composer, poet, or craftsman—and, in a small way, the same principle applies here.

Among the many who have helped us over the years, though, are a few who must be acknowledged by name because of their willingness to share the insights from their own experience, to help build homeschooling teams, co-ops, and other networks, or to sustain relationships of constant and unstinting friendship.

Our chapter on homeschooling groups discusses in some detail our involvement with Nancy Plent, founder of the Unschoolers Network, and we certainly wish to acknowledge her importance to our homeschooling. Tim Haas has helped many New Jersey families homeschool successfully, and has been a valuable source of information as well as a good friend. Brian Ray, president of the National Home Education Research Institute, gave generously of his time and expertise. Andrew Schlafly's initiatives, including his courses on various subjects, have been instrumental to many New Jersey families as they homeschool through high school.

We would like to acknowledge the inspiration derived from the homeschooling experiences of Mary Alice Landau, Carolee Adams, Haya Gray, Susan Rohrbach, Pat Fritz, Regina Ellis, Damon and Melanie Owens, and their families.

We also want to thank all of those who read various drafts of this manuscript and offered reactions, suggestions, encouragement, and other valuable guidance. Some were not homeschoolers. The first of these were William D. Falloon, a journalist, editor, and friend, and Ellen Rice, who provided a helpful recommendation about format. Later, the extraordinary writers and teachers James Alan McPherson and Tessa Rumsey were kind enough to read the penultimate draft of the manuscript and give constructive criticism. Several homeschoolers took time from their busy schedules to help us ensure that the book address thoroughly and in helpful detail all the challenges that most in homeschooling are apt to encounter. In particular, we want to thank Amy Mandelker for her careful reading and detailed feedback on the book. (Professor Mandelker's contribution to our homeschooling and that of many other New Jersey families includes her having founded the Merely Players, a homeschooling Shakespeare troupe we discuss elsewhere in the book. She has been unstinting in her willingness to share time, expertise, and enthusiasm.) We especially want to thank our trial readers, a group of current or former homeschoolers, including but not limited to Barbara Snyder, Mary Ann and James O'Toole, and Martha Nowik.

Of course, our thanks go to those whose words of praise for the book appear on the back cover.

Several groups have been critical to the success of our homeschooling efforts. We would like to acknowledge the Home School Legal Defense Association (HSLDA), which provided much-needed security, especially during the early years of our homeschooling, and which continues to be a source of information and insight. We would like to thank the other member families of the Little Way Homeschool Cooperative. We are grateful to those families who have worked with the Carpe Diem Forensics Association, and to its founding coach, Michael Chen. Some of the groups most important to our homeschooling are not, strictly speaking, homeschooling groups. We would like to thank John Daley, James Douglas, Peter Hubert, and members of the Westfield Fife and Drum Corps. Yoshisada Yonezuka, former U.S. Olympic head coach and founder of the Cranford Judo & Karate Center has been and remains both a teacher and an exemplar. The member families of the Union Chinese School welcomed us and we are grateful for their long hospitality. It was there that we began our family's relationship with Susan Cheng and Wang Guowei, executive director and artistic director, respectively, of Music from China—our thanks for the opportunity to work with that orchestra.

The staff and faculty of Raritan Valley Community College have been a valuable source of instruction, mentoring, and opportunity in many areas. We want to extend our thanks to Stephen Brower, for his ongoing cooperation in our Web presence. Raymond Mammano, formerly head of the guidance department of Watchung Hills Regional High School, surprised us with his alacrity and ability to work with homeschoolers as we were preparing our daughters for the college admissions maze.

Convention dictates that those most directly and continuously responsible for supporting a book be among the last acknowledged. We owe much to the commitment and good judgment of Mitch Horowitz, our editor at Tarcher/Penguin, and the diligence of his associate, Gabrielle Moss. Glen Hartley and Lynn Chu, of Writers Representatives, LLC, went far beyond the conventional responsibilities of a literary agency to help us negotiate a path through the shifting perplexities of the publishing industry. Thanks, Glen and Lynn.

The Reverend Robert A. Connor, philosopher, spiritual director, and friend, has made a gift of self to us for more than two decades now. Our gratitude is inexpressible—except, perhaps, in an attempt to emulate the gift itself. We are trying.

We acknowledge our children, Bridget, Anna, Magdalen, William, Joseph, and Gregory Blaise, as coauthors and editors—subjects, never objects.

Finally, we must acknowledge, though not by name, several teachers and bureaucrats who, by their determined refusal to understand, cooperate, innovate, or extend themselves in any way, vexed us so intolerably that we knew there had to be a better way. If they had not held closed the doors, we might never have looked for a window.

Notes

Introduction

1. Jane Sutton, "Home Schooling Comes of Age," *Brown Alumni Magazine,* January/February 2002.
2. Bob Egelko and Jill Tucker, "Homeschoolers' Setback Sends Shock Waves Through State," *San Francisco Chronicle,* March 7, 2008. http://www .sfgate.com/cgi-bin/article.cgi?f=/c/a/2008/03/07/MNJDVF0F1.DTL.
3. Jill Tucker and Bob Egelko, "Governor Vows to Protect Homeschooling," *San Francisco Chronicle,* March 8, 2008. http://www.sfgate.com/cgi-bin/ article.cgi?f=/c/a/2008/03/07/INCHVG0SD.DTL.
4. Bob Egelko, "California Homeschooling Case to Be Reheard," *San Francisco Chronicle,* March 27, 2008. http://www.sfgate.com/cgi-bin/ article.cgi?f=/c/a/2008/03/27/BA7CVR0TG.DTL.

One

1. Neil MacFarquhar, "Strip Search of Third Graders Prompts Prosecutor's Inquiry," *The New York Times,* October 10, 1995. http://query.nytimes.com/ gst/fullpage.html?res=990CE3D6173BF933A05757C0A963958260.

2. "The Securities Industry Association has reported that since the October 1987 crash, the securities industry has lost 33,000 jobs." "Company News: Quotron Is Set to Lay Off 400," *The New York Times,* October 31, 1989.

3. See, for example, Theodore R. Sizer. *Horace's Compromise,* third edition (New York: Houghton Mifflin, 1984; Mariner Books, 1997).

4. See, for example, Lawrence M. Rudner, "Scholastic Achievement and Demographic Characteristics of Home School Students in 1998," Educational Policy Analysis Archives, vol. 7, no. 8 (March 23, 1999), ISSN 1068-2341.

5. Arthur G. Powell, Eleanor Farrar, and David K. Cohen, National Association of Secondary School Principals (U.S.); National Association of Independent Schools Commission on Educational Reform (corporate author), *The Shopping Mall High School: Winners and Losers in the Educational Marketplace* (New York: Houghton Mifflin, 1985), p. 302.

6. Statement based on my personal experience in Catholic schools grades 1 through 12.

Two

1. Interview, June 2, 2006.

2. Patricia Albjerg Graham, *Schooling America: How the Public Schools Meet the Nation's Changing Needs* (New York: Oxford University Press, 2005), pg. 1.

3. Cited in Herbert M. Kliebard, *Schooled to Work: Vocationalism and the American Curriculum, 1876–1946* (New York: Teachers College Press, 1999), p. 229.

4. Winnie Hu, "Leaving the City for the Schools, and Regretting It," *The New York Times,* November 13, 2006.

5. Lawrence M. Rudner, "Scholastic Achievement and Demographic Characteristics of Home School Students in 1998," Educational Policy Analysis Archives, vol. 7, no. 8 (March 23, 1999), ISSN 1068-2341.

6. Richard G. Medlin, "Home Schooling and the Question of Socialization," *Peabody Journal of Education,* 75 (1&2) (2000), p. 111: "In fact, Delahooke found that home-schooled children actually participated in more activities than did children attending a conventional school."

7. Ibid., p. 112.
8. Ibid., p. 115: "The results were striking—the mean problem behavior score for children attending conventional schools was more than eight times higher than that of the home-schooled group."
9. Richard Buddin and Ron Zimmer, "Academic Outcomes," Chapter Three in *Charter School Operations and Performance: Evidence from California*, p. 56. PDF available at http://www.rand.org/pubs/monograph_reports/ MR1700/.
10. See transcript of Conference on Telephone Privacy, July 22, 1992, National Press Club, Washingon, D.C. Available through Electronic Frontier Foundation at http://www.eff.org/Privacy/?f=phone_92_privacy_conf .transcript.
11. See Brian Greene, *Fabric of the Cosmos*.
12. E.g., 38th Annual Phi Delta Kappa/Gallup Poll of the Public's Attitudes Toward the Public Schools, August 2006. Available at http://www .pdkintl.org/kappan/k0609pol.htm.

Three

1. Interview. Name and identifying details withheld at source's request.
2. For more on fear in schools, see John Holt, *How Children Fail*.
3. See Robert Kubey and Mihaly Csikszentmihalyi, "Television Addiction Is No Mere Metaphor," *Scientific American* 286 (2) (February 2002), p. 74.
4. Interview, July 20, 2006.
5. Ibid.
6. Ibid.
7. Lawrence Rudner, "Scholastic Achievement and Demographic Characteristics of Home Schooled Students in 1998." ERIC Clearinghouse on Assessment and Evaluation, College of Library and Information Services, University of Maryland, College Park. http://epaa.asu.edu/epaa/ v7n8/.
8. See Donald F. Roberts, Ulla G. Foehr, and Victoria Rideout, "Generation M: Media in the Lives of 8–18 Year Olds," A Kaiser Family Foundation Study, The Henry J. Kaiser Family Foundation. March 2005, p. 36.
9. Interview, July 20, 2006.

Four

1. David Elkind, *The Hurried Child: Growing Up Too Fast, Too Soon* (New York: Perseus, 2001), p. 38.
2. Ibid., p. 37.
3. Howard Gardner, *To Open Minds: Chinese Clues to the Dilemma of Contemporary Education* (New York: Basic Books, 1989), p. 293.
4. See Howard Gardner, *Changing Minds: The Art and Science of Changing Our Own and Other People's Minds* (Boston: Harvard Business School Press, 2004), pp. 23–49.
5. See Harry F. Harlow, "The Nature of Love," Address of the President at the Sixty-sixth Annual Convention of the American Psychological Association, Washington, D.C., August 31, 1958. First published in *American Psychologist* 13, pp. 573–685. Accessible at http://psychclassics .yorku.ca/Harlow/love.htm.
6. See N. R. Kleinfield, "The Elderly Man and the Sea?: Test Sanitizes Literary Texts," *The New York Times,* June 2, 2002. See also Diane Ravitch, *The Language Police: How Pressure Groups Restrict What Students Learn* (New York: Vintage Books, 2004).
7. Stephen R. Covey, *The Seven Habits of Highly Effective People,* p. 22.
8. See NBER Digest, September 2003. National Bureau of Economic Research Faculty Research Fellows Marianne Bertrand and Sendhil Mullainathan examined patterns of discrimination in how employers responded to names on résumés—with African-American names much less likely to get callbacks than white-sounding names. In a reflection on whether training could alleviate patterns of discrimination, the authors suggested it was rational for African-Americans to be skeptical about training. "If African Americans recognize how employers reward their skills, they may be rationally more reluctant than whites to even participate in these programs." *NBER Digest,* September, 2003, p. 2.
9. Sam Dillon, "Test Shows Drop in Science Achievement for Twelfth Graders," *The New York Times,* May 25, 2006, p. A20.
10. Christa Case, "US Lags in Math, but Not as Far," *Christian Science Monitor.* Dec. 16, 2004, p. 17.
11. See Arthur G. Powell, Eleanor Farrar, and David K. Cohen, National Association of Secondary School Principals (U.S.); National Association of Independent Schools Commission on Educational Reform (corpo-

rate author), *The Shopping Mall High School* (New York: Houghton Mifflin, 1985).

12. For a history of this movement see Herbert Kliebard, *The Struggle for the American Curriculum 1893–1953*. pp. 240–71.

13. A. H. Lauchner, "How Can the Junior High School Curriculum Be Improved?," *Bulletin of the National Association of Secondary School Principals,* 35(177) (1951): 296–304. Cited in Kliebard, *Struggle,* p. 262.

Five

1. Peter Gelling, "Reading the Menacing Ash, with Only a Wisp of Science," *The New York Times Online,* June 13, 2006.

2. Roni Rabin, "Breast-Feed or Else," *New York Times Online,* June 13, 2006.

3. Herbert Kliebard, *The Struggle for the American Curriculum 1893–1953,* p. 162.

4. See Susan Saulny, "The Gilded Age of Home Schooling," *The New York Times Online,* June 5, 2006.

5. James Surowiecki, *The Wisdom of Crowds* (New York: Doubleday, 2004), p. 70.

6. "Become who you are," a phrase first used by Pindar and later by Nietzsche, was more recently by Pope John Paul II.

7. See Frank Swoboda, "Pepsi Prank Fizzles at School's Coke Day," *Washington Post,* March 26, 1998, p. A1.

8. See GAO Reports: GAO/04-810, "Commercial Activities in Schools," August 2004, and GAO/HEHS-00-156 "Commercial Activities in Schools," September 2000. See also http://www.mediafamily.org/facts/facts_adsinschool.shtml.

9. For "selling soft drinks and junk food to students," see ibid. For cutbacks on physical education see, for example, Julie Bosman, "Putting the Gym Back in Gym Class," *The New York Times,* Oct. 13, 2005: "Today only 5.8 percent to 8 percent of schools provide what phys ed advocates recommend—gym classes five times a week—according to the Centers for Disease Control and Prevention. School administrators began cutting physical education programs decades ago, in part because of the way many classes were taught." See also Nicole Sweeney, "As Obesity

Grows, Schools Cut Physical Education: Activity Levels of Students Drop from Years Ago," *Milwaukee Journal Sentinel,* April 25, 2004.

10. GAO-05-563, "School Meal Programs: Competitive Foods Are Widely Available and Generate Substantial Revenues for Schools," August 2005.

11. Caroline Hoxby, "How Teachers' Unions Affect Educational Production," *Quarterly Journal of Economics* 111(3) (1996).

12. For an overview of No Child Left Behind by its supporters, see http://www.whitehouse.gov/news/releases/2002/01/20020108.html.

13. Interview, January 12, 2006.

14. Sam Dillon, "Schools Cut Back Subjects to Push Reading and Math," *The New York Times,* March 26, 2006.

15. Popham interview. Jan. 12, 2006.

Eight

1. Deborah Gordon, *Ants at Work: How an Insect Society Is Organized* (New York: Free Press, 1999), p. vii.

2. John H. Holland, *Emergence: From Chaos to Order* (Reading, Mass.: Addison-Wesley, 1998), p. 2.

3. See Steven Johnson, *Emergence: The Connected Lives of Ants, Brains, Cities and Software* (New York: Scribner, 2001).

4. Jane Jacobs, *The Death and Life of Great American Cities.* Cited in Johnson, ibid, p. 51.

5. Johnson, ibid., p. 41.

6. Robert D. Putnam, *Bowling Alone: The Collapse and Revival of American Community* (New York: Simon & Schuster, 2000), p. 19.

7. Ibid., p. 414.

8. Lawrence M. Rudner, "Scholastic Achievement and Demographic Characteristics of Home School Students in 1998," *Educational Policy Analysis Archives* 7 (8) (March 23, 1999).

9. Susan A. McDowell, and Brian D. Ray, "The Home Education Movement in Context, Practice and Theory: Editors' Introduction," *Peabody Journal of Education,* 75 (1&2) (2000), p. 1.

10. Richard G. Medlin, "Home Schooling and the Question of Socialization," *Peabody Journal of Education,* 75 (1&2), 2000, p. 111: "In fact, Delahooke found that home-schooled children actually participated in more activities than did children attending a conventional school."

11. Ibid., p. 112.

12. Ibid., p. 115: "The results were striking—the mean problem behavior score for children attending conventional schools was more than eight times higher than that of the home-schooled group."

13. For an examination of Taylor's influence on the school system, see Kliebard, *History of the American Curriculum.*

14. For more on emergent systems see Holland, *Emergence: From Chaos to Order,* (1997), and Johnson, *Emergence: The Connected Lives of Ants, Brains, Cities, and Software.*

15. So-called cyber charters, online schools that allow students to follow the standard school curriculum but to work online instead of in a classroom, are neither homeschooling nor unschooling. The difference between homeschooling and a cyber charter is like the difference between self-employment and telecommuting to a job.

16. See Rudner, "Scholastic Achievement." He found that nearly a fifth of the families in his research population of homeschoolers included parents with teaching certificates. Readers interested in following up on this point might also see John Holt, *How Children Fail* (New York: Perseus, 1995).

17. "On average, the certification status of a teacher has at most small impacts on student test performance." See Thomas Kane, Johah E. Rockoff, and Douglas O. Staiger, "What Does Certification Tell Us About Teacher Effectiveness?: Evidence from New York City," National Bureau of Economic Research Working Paper 12155, March 2006, p. 1.

18. Susan A. McDowell, "The Home Schooling Mother-Teacher: Toward a Theory of Social Integration," *Peabody Journal of Education* 75 (1&2), p. 201.

19. Rudner, "Scholastic Achievement," Table 2.8.

20. Ronald S. Burt, *Brokerage and Closure: An Introduction to Social Capital* (New York: Oxford University Press, 2005).

21. Caroline Minter Hoxby, "How Teachers' Unions Affect Educational Production," *Quarterly Journal of Economics* 3 (August 1996): 617–718.

Nine

1. Tom Parker (dean of admissions, Amherst), interview with author, July 25, 2006.

2. Jim Bock (dean of admissions and financial aid, Swarthmore), interview with author, July 25, 2006.
3. John Latting (director of undergraduate admissions, Johns Hopkins), interview with author, July 27, 2006.
4. Harold Wingood (associate provost, dean of admissions and financial aid, Clark University), interview with author, April 27, 2006.
5. Richard H. Shaw (dean of admissions, Stanford), interview with author, March 30, 2006.
6. John Boshoven (past president, Michigan Association of College Counselors), interview with author, May 2, 2006.
7. Angela Evans (assistant director of admissions, Kennesaw State University), interview with author, April 5, 2006.
8. Mike Donahue (admissions director, IUPUI, Indiana University/Purdue), interview with author, April 5, 2006.
9. Evans interview.
10. Bock interview.
11. Ibid.
12. Jon Reider (director of undergraduate admissions, Stanford), interview with author, April 26, 2006.
13. Ibid.
14. Ibid.
15. Ibid.
16. Ibid.
17. Shaw interview.
18. Ibid.
19. Ibid.
20. Ibid.
21. Ibid.
22. James Wrenn (professor emeritus of Asian studies, Brown), interview with author, August 8, 2006, and March 14, 2008.
23. See Sean Callaway, "Unintended Admission Consequences of Federal Aid for Homeschoolers," *The Journal of College Admissions,* Fall 2004, p. 24.
24. Evans interview.
25. Reider interview.
26. Latting interview.
27. Ted O'Neill (dean of admissions, University of Chicago), interview with author, July 31, 2006.

28. Bock interview.
29. O'Neill interview.
30. Wingood interview.
31. O'Neill interview.
32. Latting interview.
33. Bock interview.
34. See Porter, Kathleen, "The Value of a College Degree," ERIC Clearing-house on Higher Education, ERIC Digest, ERIC identifier ED470038. Available at http://www.ericdigests.org/2003-3/value.htm.
35. Dr. Paul Jones and Dr. Gene Gloeckner, "Admissions Officers' Perceptions of and Attitudes Toward Homeschool Students," *The Journal of College Admissions,* Fall 2004, p. 21.
36. Latting interview.
37. Marlyn McGrath-Lewis (director of admissions, Harvard), interview with author, April 5, 2006.
38. Wingood interview.

Bibliography

Articles

Bosman, Julie. "Putting the Gym Back in Gym Class." *The New York Times,* October 13, 2005.

Callaway, Sean. "Unintended Admission Consequences of Federal Aid for Homeschoolers." *The Journal of College Admission,* Fall 2004.

Case, Christa. "U.S. Lags in Math, but Not as Far." *Christian Science Monitor.* December 16, 2004, p. 17.

Dillon, Sam. "Schools Cut Back Subjects to Push Reading and Math." *The New York Times,* March 26, 2006. http://www.nytimes.com/2006/03/26/education/26child.html

Dillon, Sam. "Test Shows Drop in Science Achievement for Twelfth Graders." *The New York Times,* May 25, 2006, p. A20.

Doody, Angela. "Learning at Home: The Number of Homeschooled Students Attending Swarthmore Is on the Rise." *Swarthmore College Bulletin,* June 2003.

Foster, Christine. "In a Class by Themselves: A Wave of Homeschoolers Has Reached the Farm—Students with Unconventional Training and Few Formal Credentials: What Have They Got That Stanford Wants? And How Do Admission Officers Spot It?" *Stanford Magazine,* November/December 2000.

GAO Reports: GAO/04-810, "Commercial Activities in Schools," August 2004, and GAO/HEHS-00-156, "Commercial Activities in Schools," September 2000. See also http://www.mediafamily.org/facts/facts_adsinschool.shtml.

GAO-05-563 "School Meal Programs: Competitive Foods Are Widely Available and Generate Substantial Revenues for Schools," August 2005.

Gelling, Peter. "Reading the Menacing Ash, with Only a Wisp of Science." *The New York Times,* June 13, 2006.

Harlow, Harry F. "The Nature of Love." Address of the President at the Sixty-sixth Annual Convention of the American Psychological Association, Washington, D.C., August 31, 1958. First published in *American Psychologist* 13, pp. 573–685. Currently accessible online at http://psychclassics.yorku.ca/Harlow/love.htm.

Hoxby, Caroline. "How Teachers' Unions Affect Educational Production." *Quarterly Journal of Economics* 111(3) (1996).

Hu, Winnie. "Leaving the City for the Schools, and Regretting It." *The New York Times,* November 13, 2006.

Kane, Thomas, and Susan A. McDowell. "The Home Schooling Mother-Teacher: Toward a Theory of Social Integration." *Peabody Journal of Education* 75 (1&2).

Keenan, Faith, with Stanley Holmes, Jay Greene, and Roger O. Crockett. "A Mass Market of One." *Business Week,* December 2, 2002. http://www.businessweek.com/magazine/content/02_48/b3810088.htm.

Kleinfield, N. R. "The Elderly Man and the Sea?: Test Sanitizes Literary Texts." *The New York Times,* June 2, 2002.

Kubey, Robert, and Mihaly Csikszentmihalyi. "Television Addiction Is No Mere Metaphor." *Scientific American* 286 (2) (February 2002), p. 74.

Lauchner, A. H. "How Can the Junior High School Curriculum Be Improved?" *Bulletin of the National Association of Secondary School Principals,* 35(177), pp. 296–304.

MacFarquhar, Neil. "Strip Search of Third Graders Prompts Prosecutor's Inquiry." *The New York Times,* October 10, 1995. *The New York Times* Archives. http://query.nytimes.com/gst/fullpage.html?res=990CE3D6173BF933A0 5757C0A963958260.

McDowell, Susan A., and Brian D. Ray. "The Home Education Movement in Context, Practice and Theory: Editors' Introduction." *Peabody Journal of Education* 75 (1&2), (2000).

Medlin, Richard G. "Home Schooling and the Question of Socialization." *Peabody Journal of Education* 75 (1&2), (2000).

BIBLIOGRAPHY

Porter, Kathleen. "The Value of a College Degree." ERIC Clearinghouse on Higher Education, ERIC Digest, ERIC identifier ED470038. Available at http://www.ericdigests.org/2003-3/value.htm.

Rabin, Roni. "Breast-Feed or Else." *The New York Times,* June 13, 2006.

Roberts, Donald F., Ulla G. Foehr, and Victoria Rideout. "Generation M: Media in the Lives of 8–18 Year Olds." A Kaiser Family Foundation Study. The Henry J. Kaiser Family Foundation, March 2005.

Rockoff, Johah E., and Douglas O. Staiger. "What Does Certification Tell Us About Teacher Effectiveness?: Evidence from New York City." National Bureau of Economic Research Working Paper 12155, March 2006.

Rudner, Lawrence M. "Scholastic Achievement and Demographic Characteristics of Home School Students in 1998." *Education Policy Analysis Archives* 7 (8) (March 23, 1999). Available at http://epaa.asu.edu/epaa/v7n8/.

Saulny, Susan. "The Gilded Age of Home Schooling." *The New York Times,* June 5, 2006. http://www.nytimes.com/2006/06/05/education/05homeschool.html?ex=1307160000&en=80dabb4310a7fa20&ei=5088&partner=rssnyt&emc=rss.

Sutton, Jane. "Home Schooling Comes of Age." *Brown Alumni Magazine,* January/February, 2002.

Sweeney, Nicole. "As Obesity Grows, Schools Cut Physical Education: Activity Levels of Students Drop from Years Ago." *Milwaukee Journal Sentinel,* April 25, 2004. Available at http://www.jsonline.com/story/index.aspx?id=224866.

Swoboda, Frank. "Pepsi Prank Fizzles at School's Coke Day." *Washington Post,* March 26, 1998, p. A1.

Books

Bennett, William J., Chester E. Finn, Jr., and John T. E. Cribb, Jr. *The Educated Child: A Parent's Guide from Preschool Through Eighth Grade.* New York: Free Press, 1999.

Bernstein, Peter L. *Against the Gods: The Remarkable Story of Risk.* New York: John Wiley, 1996.

Bernstein, Peter L. *Capital Ideas: The Improbable Origins of Modern Wall Street.* New York: Free Press, 1992.

Buddin, Richard, and Ron Zimmer. "Academic Outcomes," Chapter Three in

Charter School Operations and Performance: Evidence from California, p. 56. PDF available at http://www.rand.org/pubs/monograph_reports/MR1700/.

Burt, Ronald S. *Brokerage and Closure: An Introduction to Social Capital*. New York: Oxford University Press, 2005.

Chalmers, David J. *The Conscious Mind: In Search of a Fundamental Theory.* New York: Oxford University Press, 1996.

Clark, Mary Kay, Ph.D. *Catholic Home Schooling: A Handbook for Parents*. Rockford, Ill.: Seton Home Study School Press, 1993.

Cohen, Cafi. *Homeschoolers' College Admissions Handbook: Preparing 12-to-18-Year-Olds for Success in the College of Their Choice*. New York: Three Rivers Press, 2000.

Cohen, Katherine, Ph.D. *The Truth About Getting In: A Top College Advisor Tells You Everything You Need to Know.* New York: Hyperion, 2002.

Colfax, David and Micki. *Homeschooling for Excellence*. New York: Warner Books, 1998.

Covey, Stephen R. *The Seven Habits of Highly Effective People*. New York: Free Press, 2004.

Crump, J. I., translated and annotated and with an introduction by. *Chan-kuo Ts'e*. Ann Arbor: Center for Chinese Studies, the University of Michigan, 1996.

Dobson, James, Ph.D. *Hide or Seek*. Pomona, Calif.: Fleming H. Revell, 1979.

Elkind, David. *The Hurried Child: Growing Up Too Fast, Too Soon*. New York: Perseus, 2001.

Elkind, David. *Miseducation: Preschoolers at Risk*. New York: Knopf, 1987.

Elster, Jon. *Alchemies of the Mind: Rationality and the Emotions*. Cambridge: Cambridge University Press, 1999.

Evans, Dylan. *Emotion: The Science of Sentiment*. New York: Oxford University Press, 2001.

Fair, Ray C. *Predicting Presidential Elections and Other Things*. Stanford, Calif.: Stanford University Press, 2002.

Fry, Timothy, OSB, editor. *The Rule of St. Benedict in English*. Collegeville, Minn.: The Order of St. Benedict, 1981.

Gardner, Howard. *Changing Minds: The Art and Science of Changing Our Own and Other People's Minds*. Boston: Harvard Business School Press, 2004.

Gardner, Howard. *To Open Minds: Chinese Clues to the Dilemma of Contemporary Education*. New York: Basic Books, 1989.

Gatto, John Taylor. *Dumbing Us Down: The Hidden Curriculum of Compulsory Schooling.* Gabriola Island, BC: New Society Publishers, 2005.

Giles, Herbert A., translated and annotated by. *San Tzu Ching Elementary Chinese.* Cambridge: 1910.

Gladwell, Malcolm. *The Tipping Point: How Little Things Can Make a Big Difference.* Boston, New York, London: Little, Brown, 2000.

Glimcher, Paul W. *Decisions, Uncertainty, and the Brain: The Science of Neuroeconomics.* Cambridge, Mass.: The MIT Press, 2003.

Gordon, Deborah. *Ants at Work: How an Insect Society Is Organized.* New York: Free Press, 1999.

Graham, Patricia Albjerg. *Schooling America: How the Public Schools Meet the Nation's Changing Needs.* New York: Oxford University Press, 2005.

Greene, Brian. *Fabric of the Cosmos: Space, Time and the Texture of Reality.* New York: Knopf, 2004.

Hegener, Mark and Helen. *The Home School Reader.* Tonasket, Wash.: Home Education Press, 1988.

Hirsch, E. D., Jr. *Cultural Literacy: What Every American Needs to Know.* Boston: Houghton Mifflin, 1987.

Holland, John H. *Emergence: From Chaos to Order.* Reading, Mass.: Addison-Wesley, 1998.

Holt, John. *How Children Fail.* New York: Perseus, 1995.

Holt, John. *Teach Your Own: A Hopeful Path for Education.* New York: Delta/Seymour Lawrence Dell, 1982.

Hughes, Chuck. *What It Really Takes to Get into the Ivy League & Other Highly Selective Colleges.* New York: McGraw-Hill, 2003.

Jacobs, Jane. *The Death and Life of Great American Cities.* New York: Random House, 2002.

Johnson, Steven. *Emergence: The Connected Lives of Ants, Brains, Cities and Software.* New York: Scribner, 2001.

Johnson, William. *Letters to Contemplatives.* Maryknoll, N.Y.: Orbis Books, 1992.

Johnston, William. *The Still Point: Reflections on Zen and Christian Mysticism.* New York: Fordham University Press, 1971.

Kavanaugh, Kieran, OCD, and Otilio Rodriguez, OCD. *The Collected Works of St. John of the Cross.* Washington, D.C.: ICS Publications, Institute of Carmelite Studies, 1979.

Kindleberger, Charles P. *A Financial History of Western Europe.* New York: Oxford University Press, 1993.

Klicka, Christopher J. *The Right Choice: The Incredible Failure of Public Education and the Rising Hope of Home Schooling*. Gresham, Ore.: Noble, 1993.

Kliebard, Herbert M. *Schooled to Work: Vocationalism and the American Curriculum, 1876–1946*. New York: Teachers College Press, 1999.

Kliebard, Herbert M. *The Struggle for the American Curriculum, 1893–1953*. New York and London: Routledge & Kegan Paul, 1987.

Kockelmans, Josef J. *Edmund Husserl's Phenomenology*. West Lafayette, Ind.: Purdue University Press, 1994.

Leach, Penelope. *Your Baby & Child: From Birth to Age Five*. New York: Knopf, 1985.

Lefevre, Edwin. *Reminiscences of a Stock Operator*. New York: John Wiley, 1994.

Lindstrom, Martin, with Patricia B. Seybold. *Brand Child: Remarkable Insights into the Minds of Today's Global Kids and Their Relationships with Brands*. London and Sterling, Vir.: Kogan Page, 2003.

Loewenstein, George, and Jon Elster. *Choice Over Time*. New York: Russell Sage Foundation, 1992.

Mackay, Charles, LL.D. *Extraordinary Popular Delusions and the Madness of Crowds*. London: Richard Bentley, 1841.

Moore, Raymond and Dorothy. *Home Grown Kids: A Practical Handbook for Teaching Your Children at Home*. Waco, Tex.: Word Books, 1981.

Nussbaum, Martha C. *Upheavals of Thought: The Intelligence of Emotions*. Cambridge: Cambridge University Press, 2003.

Pascale, Richard T., Mark Millemann, and Linda Gioja. *Surfing the Edge of Chaos*. New York: Three Rivers Press, 2000.

Pieper, Josef. *Faith, Hope, Love*. San Francisco: Ignatius Press, 1997.

Pieper, Josef. *The Four Cardinal Virtues: Prudence, Justice, Fortitude, Temperance*. Notre Dame, Ind.: University of Notre Dame Press, 2003.

Pieper, Josef. *Happiness and Contemplation*. South Bend, Ind.: St. Augustine's Press, 1998.

Pieper, Josef. *The Silence of St. Thomas: Three Essays*. South Bend, Ind.: St. Augustine's Press, 1999.

Pope, Loren. *Colleges That Change Lives: 40 Schools You Should Know About Even If You're Not a Straight-A Student*. New York: Penguin, 2000.

Powell, Arthur G., Eleanor Farrar, and David K. Cohen. National Association of Secondary School Principals (U.S.); National Association of Independent Schools Commission on Educational Reform (corporate author).

The Shopping Mall High School: Winners and Losers in the Educational Marketplace. New York: Houghton Mifflin, 1985.

Putnam, Robert D. *Bowling Alone: The Collapse and Revival of American Community.* New York: Simon & Schuster, 2000.

Quart, Alissa. *Branded: The Buying and Selling of Teenagers.* New York: Basic Books, 2003.

Ravitch, Diane. *The Language Police: How Pressure Groups Restrict What Students Learn.* New York: Vintage Books, 2004.

Schneider, Zola Dincin. *Campus Visits & College Interviews: A Complete Guide for College-Bound Students and Their Families.* New York: College Board, 2002.

Sizer, Theodore R. *Horace's Compromise.* New York: Houghton Mifflin, 1984; third edition: Mariner Books, 1997.

Sokolowski, Robert. *Introduction to Phenomenology.* Cambridge: Cambridge University Press, 2000.

Spiegelberg, Herbert. *The Phenomenological Movement: A Historical Introduction.* Dordrecht, Boston, London: Kluwer, 1994.

Steinberg, Jacques. *The Gatekeepers: Inside the Admissions Process of a Premier College.* New York: Viking, 2002.

Surowiecki, James. *The Wisdom of Crowds.* New York: Doubleday, 2004.

Thaler, Richard H. *Quasi Rational Economics.* New York: Russell Sage Foundation, 1991.

Waltham, Clae, arranged from the work of James Legge by. *Chuang Tzu: Genius of the Absurd.* New York: Ace Books, 1971.

Wegner, Daniel M. *The Illusion of Conscious Will.* Cambridge, Mass.: The MIT Press, 2002.

Wise, Jesse, and Bauer, Susan Wise. *The Well-Trained Mind: A Guide to Classical Education at Home.* New York: Norton, 1999.

Index

About the Authors

Martine P. Millman earned her B.A. in English in 1977 from Kenyon College. She later studied Chinese in Hong Kong and Taiwan, and worked as a writer and editor there and in New York until shortly after her marriage in 1984. Since 1985, she has dedicated most of her time to motherhood and homeschooling.

Gregory J. Millman earned MBA and M.A. (Asian Studies) degrees from Washington University in 1980, then worked in journalism, banking, consulting, and project development in Asia, Latin America, and North America. He returned to journalism in 1987 and has freelanced ever since. He was elected a Fellow of the Alicia Patterson Foundation in 1992. His previous books include *The Floating Battlefield: Corporate Strategies in the Currency Wars, The Vandals' Crown: How Rebel Currency Traders Overthrew the World's Central Banks,* and *The Day Traders: The Untold Story of the Extreme Investors and How They Changed Wall Street Forever.*